A STRAIGHTFORWARD GUIDE TO GETTING THE BEST OUT OF YOUR RETIREMENT

MAXIMISING THE BENEFIT OF YOUR RETIREMENT YEARS

PATRICK GRANT

Editor: Roger Sproston

Straightforward Publishing
www.straightforwardbooks.co.uk

Straightforward Guides

© Straightforward Co Ltd 2023

ISBN
978-1-80236-227-5

Printed by 4edge Co Ltd www.4edge.co.uk.

Cover design by Straightforward Graphics

Contents

Part Two: Finances After Retirement-Pensions

****

Introduction

Most people start to seriously think about their retirement when they reach their late 50's /early 60's. They think about how they can afford their retirement and how they can best spend their time. On average, a third of a person's lifetime is spent in retirement and it is a great opportunity to take up the many things that you have not had the time for.

Future planning

Of course, it is the case that many people have a very clear idea about what they want to do and how much it is all going to cost. There is suddenly time to do everything that you have wanted, within reason and within financial limits. There are, however, hidden problems that can surface when a person retires. One of these is personal relationships. Retirement can cause stress in people's relationships as you now spend a lot more time together or one partner retires and wants to embark on different projects whilst the other is still working.

People who live alone may worry about losing the day-to-day companionship that goes with the workplace. People also worry about how they may cope as they get older and ill health begins to surface.

At the time of writing, there is the spectre of a cost-of-living crisis which has affected crucial areas such as accommodation costs and food prices. This can be particularly pertinent to older people as income reduces (in most cases). Pre-retirement, effective pension planning is crucial to ensure a comfortable standard of living is maintained.

This book updated to **2023**, attempts to cover all areas relating to retirement. The first chapters deal with more personal matters, including management of the home and future care options whilst the latter chapters deal with more financial issues, such as pensions and benefits. All in all, the reader will benefit from this highly readable book which is packed with information.

Patrick Grant
2023

****

Ch. 1

When You Retire

Although people generally look forward to retirement, it is true to say that, in the absence of any grand plans, the experience of being at home can take some adjusting to, although this is not always the case for people who are very active and easily adjust to the many opportunities afforded by finishing work.

For sure, 'retirement' does not mean that you do nothing. On the contrary, it means that you fill your time with other things that you couldn't do when you were working.

Being on your own

There are increasing numbers of people who find themselves alone when they retire. Many people like being single and have planned their lives around this. Although it is true that having a partner can mean that you have someone to be with, go on holiday with and do many other things with, some people like to do these things either on their own or perhaps with another member of the family.

However, many people on their own also hope that they can find a partner in retirement, someone to share life with. This can be more difficult for women than men. Older women outnumber men, and men may be on the lookout for a younger partner.

The truth is that, in older age, many people will find it difficult to find a partner. The opportunities get less and less. One option is to enrol on a dating site online or to go to a dating agency. If you are thinking about contacting a dating agency, particularly for the first time, make sure that you know exactly what you are looking for-a long term relationship or something less committed. Also, beware! As with many things there are a lot of bogus online dating agencies around. Make sure that you do your research well.

If you live alone, and don't intend to look for a partner, then you might want to develop your ties in the community. A sense of belonging, of community, is very important so as not to get too isolated and so as to ensure that someone will always look out for you.

Your partner

If you are retiring and have a partner, you will need to involve them in your retirement plans. This may sound obvious but by no means do all people communicate with each other clearly when it comes to life after retirement and problems can occur. You will have to decide how to cope being with each other all the time, after spending so much time apart when working. If you think that you may need help with the transition to retirement then you should contact RELATE who specialise in this area. Many people see RELATE as dealing only with marital breakdown but they specialise in marital problems generally, or potential problems. See useful addresses at the back of this book.

Sexual relations

It doesn't follow that, as people get older so their sex life diminishes or the desire goes away. It is a fact that many people enjoy active sexual relations for many years after they retire. This aspect of life is just as important to older people as for younger couples.

Most people can enjoy sexual relations throughout their lives. However, when people get older sexual expression can take many forms. The importance of an orgasm, for example, may diminish. The main thing is that two people enjoy sex in their own way. As long as fulfilment is gained then this is all that matters. Growing older can bring some advantages in relation to sex. Once a woman is past the menopause then the fear of getting pregnant disappears. For many women, the fact that their partner takes longer to reach orgasm is a definite bonus. Also, when people enter the phase of retirement there is generally more time to enjoy and explore sexual relations. It goes without saying that sexual relationships don't just involve women. Partners of the same sex equally enjoy sexual relationships as they get older.

Enhancing your sex life

Although, as discussed, people of all ages enjoy active sex lives, it is true to say that for some older people sex becomes less and less frequent. Some people eventually give up altogether, for a variety of reasons, the main one being the loss of interest in one's partner. This should also be handled in the right way. Life together doesn't have to be dominated by sex. If both parties

9

feel comfortable without sex, then so be it. The important thing is to maintain good relationships.

There are, however, a few tips which may help stimulate your sex life. A complete change of scene can be exciting. Making love in a hotel room, making love at different times of the day, watching a film can all be aides to a better sex life. You might also want to consider sexual therapy, such as Sensate Focusing, which was pioneered in America by Masters and Johnson. The treatment consists of three phases. During the first phase the couple will be tactile, told to stroke each other's bodies, apart from the genitals, telling each other what they like or dislike. At this stage, the therapist will recommend that there is no sexual intercourse. The second stage allows genital stimulation and the third stage full intercourse. If you feel that you would like to explore sexual therapy more, either through the NHS or privately you should contact the British Association for Sexual and Marital Therapy, (BASMT) www.basmt.org.uk address at the end of the book.

Age UK also has a publication called Intimate Relations: Living and Loving in Later Life.

Opportunities Available

When you retire you will find that you have a lot more time on your hands, and it is yours to do as you choose. There are many opportunities. People retiring today live longer and will spend, or could spend, almost as much time retired as working. The fact that you will have so much time in retirement means that it is very important that you make the best use of it.

Learning opportunities

When you are retired you can set your goals however you want and one very useful way to use your time is to embark on a course of learning. You can study for your own personal satisfaction, studying, for example, politics and current affairs, philosophy, or information technology. You may want to study informally or to obtain specific qualifications, such as GCSE. Another aspect of attending classes, either in the day or in the evening is that you will meet like-minded people.

Because of age discrimination legislation contained within the 2010 Equalities Act, colleges and universities cannot refuse people entry to courses on the grounds of age, so the opportunities are limitless.

Informal ways of learning
Libraries
Libraries are a good place to find out what courses are happening in your area. Many libraries have also set up open learning centres where access to computers and the Internet is free, or at a very low cost.

Museums and galleries
As well as visiting museums and galleries you will also find that you can attend courses, lectures and various events organised by their education department for interested adults.

Radio and Television
Many radio and TV programmes are educational and certain programmes are dedicated to education, such as the Discovery

channel. The Open University also has some very interesting programmes, based around their curriculum.

The Internet

This is, without doubt, a very convenient way to learn with almost every subject under the sun being available. If you are experienced and have used the Internet, and almost everyone has nowadays, then you will have access to a rich variety of subjects.

If you are new to computers and would like to enrol on a course to learn more, you should try to find the one that best suits your needs. You might want to contact Digital Unite which is an organisation that offers computer training to the over 50's. It has a national network of older trainers:
www.digitalunite.com 0800 228 9272

In addition, many Age UK groups and organisations offer Internet and computer taster sessions in various community locations. You can contact Age UK's information line 0800 678 1602 or see the website www.ageuk.org.uk.

Attending classes locally

One of the most beneficial ways of learning is to attend a class near your home. There are a variety of classes, run by Local authority adult education services, Worker Educational Associations and others. The University of the Third Age is a useful organisation where activities are all arranged by members themselves, often being carried out in people's homes. The term 'university' is misleading, as no qualifications and exams are involved. There are more than 500 groups in the UK (see useful addresses at the back of the book). Learn Direct can also provide useful information about all areas of education and learning. You should phone 01202 006464 for more information or go onto their website www.learndirect.com.

Learning away from home

If you are not interested in committing yourself to a longer course then there is also the option of short residential courses, providing you can afford the fees. There are a variety of courses, from summer schools in colleges or universities and also field study centres. You can find information in local papers, travel agencies or in the Time to Learn Directory for which you have to pay. This is published twice a year by City and Guilds (see useful addresses at rear of book) or available online.

The Learning and Work Institute www.learningandwork.org.uk also offers useful information (see useful addresses).

Distance learning

'Distance learning' refers to learning by post, radio, email, television, or, as is usually the case, the Internet. Although not everyone's cup of tea, it can be a useful form of learning. The main advantage is the flexibility as regards the contents and duration of the course. The Open University www.open.ac.uk is perhaps the most famous of the distance learning organisations, where you can study for a degree (or not). The University offers a vast range of courses. See useful addresses for more information. The Open College of the Arts www.oca.ac.uk provides home study courses in a wide range of arts subjects, including music, photography and creative writing. The National

Extension College (NEC) www.nec.ac.uk offers a wide variety of courses-from maths to bird watching including courses specifically geared to the needs of people who left school without qualifications and have not studied for some time, if at all.

The Association of Distance Learning Colleges www.adlc.org.uk can provide lists of colleges and courses. For all the above see useful addresses at the end of the book. For general information on distance learning courses, or to check the credentials of a course provider, contact the Open and Distance Learning Quality Council (ODLQC) www.odlqc.org.uk See useful addresses. In Scotland you should visit: www.skillsdevelopmentscotland.co.uk

Taking a degree
Many universities and colleges will accept mature students based on their experience rather than any formal paper qualifications. Many universities and colleges have foundation courses which can be taken prior to enrolling for a degree course. You will need to pay fees for taking a degree although if you are on a low income then you may qualify for assistance. Students of any age may apply for a student loan to help with tuition fees. However, you can only get a loan to help with living costs if you are under 60 years of age (England and Wales). In Scotland there are no fees for students: www.mygov.scot/tuition-fee

The government website www.direct.gov.uk has helpful information about financing adult learning. General information about funding and concessions is available from Learndirect at www.learndirect.com.

For most people enrolling at the Open University, there is no need for any prior qualifications. However, OU students do not qualify for grants. An OU degree will usually take a little longer than a full-time university-based degree because of the nature of the learning process. It can take between 4-6 years to complete although this is dependent on the individual student.

For more information go to the OU website www.open.ac.uk or phone 0300 303 5303.

Getting involved in the community

Whilst people are at work, time for getting involved in community activities is limited. However, when you reach retirement age, there is adequate opportunity to get involved. Becoming involved in the local community can be very rewarding indeed and can be life changing in terms of who you meet and the activities that you get involved in.

Joining a local club or society

The best source of information concerning the type of club and the whereabouts is the local library. Before committing yourself to join any club you should take a look at the programme and attend an initial meeting as a guest. This will help you get an idea of the club/societies activities and to make a decision whether you want to give more of your time. Once involved you will meet many people with similar interests as you and this can be very rewarding.

Clubs for older people

Many of the larger employers will run clubs for ex-employees. These might be the civil service or NHS for example. Local Age UK's will provide information about different clubs and societies. In addition, active older people are always required as volunteers.

Women's clubs

The traditional idea of the women's institute, that of elderly and stuffy people is no longer anywhere near the truth. Today's WIs are very stimulating and can offer a range of activities for members. If you want more information, contact the National Federation of Women's Institutes www. thewi.org.uk

Working as a volunteer

If you have the energy and the time then working as a volunteer can be very rewarding indeed. It can enable you to put to good use the skills that you have acquired at work, and to keep your hand in. Alternatively, it can give you the opportunity to do something totally different. The opportunities for doing voluntary work are endless. The following gives you some idea of the range of volunteering jobs. You could:

- Act as a guide or steward in a museum or stately home- the National Trust is always in need of volunteers.
- Train to be a counsellor for organisations such as Relate, the Salvation Army or Victim Support.
- Work with children and young people in a variety of settings.
- Work with older people.

- Help run a charity shop.
- Become an advocate for a Citizens Advice Bureau.
- Become a magistrate or local councillor.
- Sit on tribunals.
- Participate in governing bodies such as a school governing body.

You need to think about what you have to offer and what you really want to do and how much time you want to devote to voluntary work. As stated, it can be a very rewarding experience. You can find voluntary work through a variety of different mediums, such as Age Concern, libraries,

The National Association For Voluntary and Community action (NAVCA), www.navca.org.uk volunteer centres, REACH, www.reachskill.org.uk (which recruits volunteers with managerial and technical backgrounds) (see useful addresses) and the Retired and Senior Volunteer Programme www.csv-rsvp.org.uk which recruits volunteers over the age of 50. For more information about VSO (Volunteering Overseas) www.vso.org.uk see useful addresses. WORKING FOR A CHARITY www.wfac.org.uk offers training courses for people who want to volunteer in the charitable sector. See useful addresses.

****

Ch. 2

Taking Holidays

For most people who are working, holidays are confined to a few weeks a year. For those with children, holidays are usually limited to school holidays. However, once you are retired, money permitting, the choices are that much greater. There is more freedom and flexibility to plan holidays around off-peak times and to stay away longer.

In addition, your priorities may change. Whereas when holidays were limited to a few weeks a year, sun, sand and sea may have been the destination. The possibilities are greater when you are retired.

The various holidays available
Activity holidays

In retirement you may be looking for something more stimulating than lying around on a beach (not that all people do that). Activity holidays have a special appeal and there are a number of possibilities.

Special-interest holidays

These are run by many operators. Details can be found in various media, such as special interest magazines or from Tourist

Boards, Tourist Information Centres or from travel agents. These holidays cover a whole range of activities, including, for example, sports holidays, arts and crafts, outdoor pursuits, from canoeing to potholing, history tours, cooking, music and languages. These are just a few. There will almost certainly be something for everyone. Another option may be working holidays and the Conservation Volunteers www.greentraveller.co.uk is one example of an organisation that runs working holidays.

Town twinning exchanges with European counterpart towns are organised by local groups. If the town that you live in has a European Twin (or any other twin for that matter) you should approach your local council for more details. This is also temporarily affected by the pandemic.

Cycling holidays are one of the best ways to explore the countryside. Cycling has become even more popular during the pandemic. Careful planning is needed here because obviously a lot will depend on your own personal capacity. Look at maps to ensure that you choose a route that isn't littered with steep hills. The National Cycling Charity, Cycling UK, www.cyclinguk. org. can provide information on cycling tours and routes in this country and abroad.

Walking holidays are another good way to see the countryside. The Ramblers Association www.ramblers.org.uk offer walking holidays. All holidays are carefully graded, ranging from the easy to the hard. The Ramblers can also assist if you would like a walking companion. Walking Women www.walkingwomen.com (see useful addresses) arranges women's walking holidays in the UK and abroad. Many women decide to go on their own. The site offers useful advice on walking holidays and the pandemic.

Reunion holidays are well worth considering if you have relatives abroad. It might be worth joining a 'friendship club' – membership of Lion World Travel/Friendship Associations, for example, www.friendship-associations.co.uk entitles you to newsletters and discount flights for reunions in Australia, South Africa and New Zealand.

Specialist tour operators

There are a growing number of tour operators offering specialist holidays for older people. Many of these are online and can be cheaper than the traditional operators. Also, local Age UK organisations and other groups run their own holidays, usually for more active older people.

Holidays for the single person

As we all know, on many fronts' holidays can pose a number of problems for the single traveller. The main one, of course, is the absence of a companion. However, many holiday prices are built around two people travelling. The single person supplement can add a significant amount to a holiday. One way around this is to go on an activity holiday, as detailed above. However, this isn't the ideal solution if you enjoy travelling around at your own pace on an itinerary designed by you. One company, justyou.co.uk offers holidays for weekends and longer breaks. There are also other companies that offer singles holidays and these can be best sourced online.

Long-stay holidays

Again, long stay holidays are subject to travel restrictions. When things get back to normal it is worth noting that they are best taken when everyone else is working. They are cheaper and less overrun in these periods. April, May, September and October are the best months. Some special long-stay holidays are available during the winter months often at very cheap rates. A long-stay package may be the best option if it is the first time that you are embarking on such a holiday. It can also be a good bet if you are considering relocating abroad and want a taste of the country that you intend moving to. Some package holidays offer a substantial package of daytime activities and other excursions and also evening entertainment. You could take a car and rent a cottage or farmhouse in a village or right out in the country. Many holiday companies offer such packages to suit your needs.

Arranging your own holiday

If you are independent and prefer to stay that way then arranging your own holiday is obviously the best way to ensure that you can suit yourself.

Finding your own accommodation can be done as you go but it is better if you can plan in advance and book in advance. Again, arranging your own holiday can give you an insight into a place that you are thinking of moving to.

Home swapping

If you like the idea of a long stay holiday but can't really afford it, then home swapping may be a solution. You live in someone else's home for an agreed period, while they live in yours. When you arrange a swap, it is necessary to make certain arrangements, such as:

- Sort out who pays gas, electricity and phone bills, and also practicalities such as food in the freezer.
- Check the position with your insurance company regarding house contents whilst the visitors are living in the house.
- Leave instructions for domestic appliances and also other information about local buses, shops and facilities.
- Leave instructions concerning contacting contractors such as electricians, plumbers etc.
- Arrange for a neighbour to drop in and make sure all is well.

Try https://www.homeswapper.co.uk, and there are many more.

Voluntary work abroad

Another cheap way to have a long-stay holiday, when travel restrictions are lifted, is to work abroad as a volunteer. Voluntary Services Overseas (VSO) takes volunteers up to the age of 75 years old. The usual spell abroad is two years. See useful addresses for more information.

Camping and caravanning

Camping and caravanning is very popular and offers greater flexibility when travelling around. This is just the sort of freedom that many people want. It also can work out cheaper in the long run once you have invested in all the equipment. If you have never been camping or caravanning, it is better to try a short package holiday first. Many people, in a fit of enthusiasm, have invested in expensive equipment only to never use it again. The same goes with camper vans. Always hire to begin with to see whether it is for you or not. If you enjoy the experience of camping or caravanning then you can always join the Camping and Caravan Club www.campingandcaravaningclub.co.uk

Medical care abroad

It is important, if you intend to travel abroad at some point, that you are well aware of the healthcare situation in respective countries. You will need to check with your own doctor about the vaccinations that may be needed in different countries. You are covered by the NHS for medical treatment only while you are in the UK. If you fall ill whilst you are on holiday abroad, you may have to pay all or part of the cost of treatment. Obviously, medical insurance is a must. As a result of BREXIT, you now need to check healthcare arrangements in whatever country you intend to travel to. If you intend to travel in Europe you should go to www.gov.uk/guidance/uk-residents-visiting-the-eueea.

Insurance

Holiday insurance should be taken out at the time that the holiday is booked because most companies give some cover in the event of cancellation. It may be harder to get insurance as you get older, as some companies impose terms or restrict insurance for those over 70. In addition, in these times of COVID, even though we are post-pandemic, you will need to be extra vigilant and ensure your policy covers everything. You need to shop around a range of insurers to get the best deal. You should make sure that you get all the cover that you need. Information about travel and holiday insurance is available on the Association of British Insurers (ABI) website www.abi.org.uk. Advice on taking a vehicle abroad is available from the AA or RAC.

Home security while you are away

In the ideal world you will not want to give the impression that your house is unoccupied. This is an invitation to burglars.

There are certain clues that can indicate an absent owner such as:

- Uncut grass
- Junk mail and free newspapers stuck in a letterbox.

There is no real substitute for getting someone to keep an eye on your house for you. You can also use a 'home-sitting' service to look after your home whilst you are away. Always tell the insurance company that covers your property if you are going to be away for more than a few weeks. It may insist on extra security precautions if cover is to be maintained.

Can you afford a holiday?

There may be the possibility that you cannot afford a holiday. However, there may be some help available. Your local Age UK, local authority or Citizens Advice Bureau might know about charities in your area that can help.

Holidays for people with disabilities

There are a number of organisations that offer help to disabled people who are planning a holiday: www.tourismforall.co.uk is a charity that gives free information and advice on holidays for people with disabilities (see useful addresses)

- Local Age UKs sometimes organise holidays specifically for people who are frail or with disabilities.
- Local authority social services departments sometimes have their own accommodation for older and disabled people.
- The Royal Association for Disability Rights publishes a holiday guide Holidays in Britain and Ireland (see useful addresses)
- Charities such as Arthritis Care www.arthritiscare.org.uk and the Multiple Sclerosis Society www.mssociety.org.uk, for example, often provide information on holidays, and some have their own holiday homes or organise holidays for special groups.

Holidays for carers

If you are a carer and want a holiday break, it may be possible for a bed to be found in a hospital or local authority care home for the person that you care for. Ask your GP or local social services department. If you need a break yourself you can ask for a carers assessment. Vouchers may be available from the local authority to assist with the cost of care while you have your break. For more information contact Carers UK (see useful addresses).

Ch. 3

Managing Your Home

It is advisable, when reaching retirement age, to carry out an examination of the home that you live in You may decide that the home that you live in will not be suitable in the future and you may want to change, probably to something smaller or in an area where you would rather be. It could even eventually be abroad. There is also the option of moving to a care home, or housing for older people. All these options will be explored here. In addition, housing options for those with limited capital will be explored.

In many cases, those who retire and are considering selling their home will have lived in the property for many years, often raising children there. Over the years, many contacts and friendships will have formed in the community. Therefore, a number of questions need to be asked when considering selling up and moving, or giving up a rented home and moving:

- Do you still have an affinity to the area and is it likely to change in the future?
- Are you still near relatives and friends or have these patterns of friendship changed over the years and have your relatives moved on?
- Is your home expensive to run and maintain? How will this affect your finances in the future as you reach retiring age?

By releasing capital through the sale of your home and downsizing/moving area will this help your finances in the future? The sale of a larger home and the purchase of a smaller property or renting of a more age specific property can release capital which can be utilised as part of your pension plan or for liquid capital to give you a better quality of life in your retirement. If you do decide to make a move then there are also a few important points to consider:

- Will the property be easy to convert as your needs change with age?
- Is the area that you are moving to convenient in terms of amenities, doctors, hospitals etc?
- Is the area quiet in the daytime or is it noisy?
- Is the property secure?

It may well be worth doing an analysis of the good and bad points of your current home before making any decision. Of course, it may well be that, notwithstanding the good points of your current home, it is simply too large to continue to occupy, too expensive and a move is essential. When making your decision, it is well worth looking at Housing Options for Older People (HOOP) www.housingcare.org which is a self-assessment form for people wondering whether to move. The form is available from the Elderly Accommodation Council www.eac.org.uk (see useful addresses)

Moving to retirement housing
As we all know, retirement housing was hit very badly during the pandemic. Now, because of the cost-of-living crisis,

accommodation costs have increased. However, things seem to be stabilising and this is one option that you may well want to consider.

Retirement housing falls into several categories depending on need. It is usually available for those over 60, although there are a number of schemes which are designed for the over 55's. These schemes usually comprise of a number of flats, some with a resident warden, most with an alarm system connected to a central base which can summon help in the event of an emergency.

There are many different types of schemes. You basically get what you pay for and those with a number of services will have a corresponding service charge to match.

Many schemes will have a communal laundry and, in some cases, a kitchen and dining room where meals can be purchased. A guest room is also usually available.

You may decide that sheltered housing (as it is usually referred to) is the ideal choice for you. The presence of a scheme manager might be reassuring and the company of others in a communal area may suit you. However, before deciding on this option, you need to weigh up the advantages and disadvantages of more sheltered housing. There will be the feeling of being 'herded' together and the loss of independence. If you feel like this you should also see whether you can receive the range of services offered in sheltered housing in your own home.

Renting retirement housing

Most retirement homes for rent are provided by local authorities and housing associations, although not all. There are also a number of schemes offered by the larger private providers although they have to manage to high standards set by local authorities. The Elderly Accommodation Counsel can offer advice.

Purchasing a retirement home

Retirement housing for sale is usually constructed by private developers although an increasing number of housing associations are also providing this type of accommodation now. Once all the properties in a scheme have been sold then the management of the scheme will be handed over to a private management company or housing association. The management organisation will be responsible for the overall management and service provision. Most retirement homes are sold on a leasehold basis with an annual ground rent (typically £250 per annum) and with a service charge that will depend on what services you are being provided. These can range from skeletal to intensive depending on your requirements.

When purchasing a retirement home, it is always wise to buy off a developer who is registered with the National House Building Council (NHBC). The NHBC has a code of practice applying to all retirement homes built after 1st April 1990. If you are seriously considering buying into, or renting retirement housing there are a number of important points to consider:

- As with all housing, is the property in a convenient location and will it cater for your needs when you get older?
- What are the facilities within the scheme?

- Will the new property take your existing furniture or will you have to sell this and buy new?
- Most important, are the managing agents experienced in managing retirement housing?
- Who runs the management association, will leaseholders have a say in running it?
- How much is the service charge and what does it cover?
- What is the ground rent?
- What are the other expenses involved?
- If there is a separate sinking fund for future major repairs how do residents contribute to it?
- What are the arrangements for resale?
- Does the lease cover what will happen if your health deteriorates whilst you are in the property?
- Who owns the freehold of the property?

The above questions should be answered by the information provided in the Purchasers Information Pack which must be provided. The NHBC Code of Practice sets out what information should be in the pack.

Although many basic rights of leaseholders have been developed over the years and are enshrined in law, the lease is still paramount in terms of what services you will receive, how they are provided and what they will cost.

Invaluable advice for those living in, or intending to move into, retirement housing is provided by First Stop www.firststopcareadvice.org.uk See useful addresses. First Stop provides useful written information, prepared in conjunction with The Leasehold Advisory Service called Leasehold Retirement Housing, Your Rights and Remedies.

Options for people with limited resources

Most retirement housing is sold, as with other housing, at full market value. It follows that when you sell you get the current market value. When you sell your own property and look for retirement housing, you might find yourself in a position of not being able to buy elsewhere. This has particularly been the case in the last few years of spiralling house prices and the general distortions of the British housing scene. If you are in the position of not being able to buy elsewhere after selling your home, there are a few options to consider.

Shared ownership housing

Some housing associations and, increasingly due to over-development, private developers, run schemes where you can part buy and part-rent. There are all sorts of names used to describe this model, such as homebuy:
www.homebuyservice.co.uk

Essentially it is what it always has been, shared ownership. In this case, you buy a percentage of the value of the property, say 25%, and then you rent the other 75%. On top of this there will be a service charge (with flats and some houses). It is not the cheapest way to obtain housing but it ensures that you get your foot on the property ladder. You should make enquiries of your local housing association which will point you in the right direction.

Lifetime lease

Some companies offer a lifetime lease, or occupancy, which means that you buy the right to live in your home for the rest of your life. The properties are sold below the market price but you will probably get very little back if you need to move again. They are also known as life interest plans.

To find out if there are any schemes in your area you should contact your local council or the Elderly Accommodation Council (address at back of this book).

Moving to rented accommodation

If you wish to move home but cannot afford to buy elsewhere, then renting privately is another option. Rented accommodation is provided in the main by local authorities, housing associations and the private sector. It is easier to rent privately than through the public sector as there is quite often a long waiting list for property and your capital may rule you out. However, tenancies in the private sector are usually insecure in that they are let out on assured shorthold tenancies which usually have a fixed duration of six months. If you wish to rent privately you should always try to go for a minimum term of twelve months. Property investors who are holding onto property for a longer term will usually be willing to do this as they are always on the lookout for a good tenant who will pay their rent.

Remember, from June 1st, 2019, lettings agents and landlords are not allowed to charge fees when letting property, although there are certain fees a landlord can charge during the course of a tenancy.

Also, tenants' deposits are capped at 5 weeks. For more information on this area go to www.arla.co.uk/letting-agent-fees.asp

Options for existing public sector tenants
If you are already a local authority or housing association tenant, and wish to relocate to another area, you may be able to exchange your home with another council or association tenant. This will be dependant on whether the exchange is suitable, taking into account the size of the respective properties or whether any possession orders or rent arrears exist. The council or association cannot unreasonably refuse the exchange. You will find details of exchange schemes at your local council or by making enquiries to your local housing association. The Internet also has details of several national exchange schemes.

Right to buy
If you have been a council tenant for five years or more you will usually have the right to purchase your property at a discount. The discounts are now more generous, at the time of writing. You won't usually be entitled to buy your home if you are a housing association tenant, although there are some exceptions such as stock transfers from local authorities to associations where the right to buy is preserved. In addition, the current government has promised to extend right to buy to housing association tenants, although at the time of writing this hasn't happened. You won't, however, be able to exercise the right to buy in housing that is exclusively reserved for elderly people.

Moving to specialist housing

People who are finding it difficult to manage on their own may prefer to move to some sort of specialist housing. In addition to retirement or sheltered housing which has been outlined, there are various types of special housing to suit differing needs.

Extra care retirement housing

Some local councils and housing associations provide sheltered housing that provides extra levels of care. This housing is for people who need personal care services, such as help with dressing or bathing. This accommodation is usually provided in flats and there will normally be a shared lounge and dining rooms where meals are available. Housing in this category is usually run jointly with local authorities and people are placed there after a social services assessment. For more information on such schemes, you should contact the Elderly Accommodation Council

Almshouses

Almshouses are run by charitable trusts and in turn provide accommodation for older people. Each charity will have its own rules about the types of people that they house. A few almshouses can provide extra care for vulnerable residents. Residents, as the beneficiaries of charity, do not have the same legal rights as other tenants. The individuals' rights will be outlined in a 'letter of appointment' provided by the trustees or the clerk to the trustees. For more information on Almshouses, contacts the Almshouses Association, www.almshouses.org address at the back of this book.

Abbeyfield houses

Abbeyfield provides housing for people in need of sheltered accommodation. Usually this will consist of unfurnished bedsits with shared lounges, dining rooms and a shared garden. The weekly charge will include two meals a day, prepared by a resident housekeeper and facilities for residents to prepare their own breakfasts and also snacks during the day. Typically, an Abbeyfield resident will be over 75 who is supported by a network of local volunteers. Further details can be obtained from the Abbeyfield Society address at the back of the book.

Housing for those with a disability

Many councils and associations have properties which have been specially designed for people with disabilities. This is referred to as mobility or wheelchair housing. In addition, grants are available for converting existing with disabled access. Councils and housing associations also now build what is known as lifetime homes which are designed to be adapted to peoples needs as they get older.

Living with a relative

If you are thinking of moving in with a relative, or a friend, or if you are thinking of having an older relative live with you, you should always weigh up the pros and the cons of such a move. Some of the things to consider are:

- How well will you get on with the person under the same roof?
- Is there enough space?

- Will a downstairs bedroom be needed?
- Is the housing conveniently situated?
- What are the financial arrangements?
- What are the practical arrangements, such as cooking and washing?
- What would be the implications if you or your relative needed extra care?

You should also speak to your local benefits office about the implications for benefits received when you have made the move.

Moving abroad

Many people dream of leaving the UK and moving to a warmer climate when they have retired. However, both the climate due to the pandemic and also the financial climate has changed significantly in the last few years and thorough research is necessary before contemplating such a move. Many people have moved away, particularly to places like Spain, and have returned after a few years, either disillusioned or lonely or having lost money on a property that they have purchased. The situation following BREXIT has further complicated the situation.

It is easy to make enquiries about residency requirements in the various countries. The Foreign and Commonwealth office can provide information and contact details for the relevant consulates or embassies in the various countries. However, before even contemplating such a move, there are various questions that you need to address:

- Can you afford to move to another country? You have to be very clear about your financial situation in retirement. House prices abroad may seem cheap compared to the UK. However, the process of buying can be complicated and some countries, such as Spain, can be problematic, particularly now after BREXIT.
- You will need to think carefully about pension rights and health costs abroad, particularly after BREXIT.
- What about possessions? You will need specialist advice about furniture and so on, and the costs of moving.
- Can you take pets? You should always ask a vet's advice first. The Pet Travel Scheme (PETS) allows dogs and cats to re-enter the UK from certain countries without quarantine as long as they meet certain conditions. You can get further information from the Department for Environment, Food and Rural Affairs' PETS Helpline www.defra.gov.uk
- Will you want to find work? You will need professional advice about work permits in the respective countries.

Buying a property abroad
There are property magazines covering homes for sale or rent. Also, property developers are represented at retirement exhibitions. However, a word of caution, you will certainly need professional advice before embarking on a property purchase. It might be useful to buy a book on purchasing a property abroad. You will find case studies of people who have bought successfully and others who have had bad experience. For certain you will need to do your homework well. There are UK

firms of solicitors who specialise in the purchase of property abroad. Addresses for such solicitors can typically be found on the Internet.

Repairs and Improvements to your own home

One of the most important elements of your home is that of its condition. When you retire or are close to retiring, this presents the ideal opportunity to assess the overall condition of your home and to draw up a condition survey (or have one drawn up) so that you can plan expenditure. It is wise to commence the work as soon as possible after retirement, or before if possible, so that you can still carry out works yourself, without resorting to using building firms. This will save money and mean that you have more control. This chapter also points the way to the various agencies that exist which will give you advice on repairs and maintenance and funding.

Deciding what needs to be carried out

There are specialist advice agencies, called Home Improvement Agencies (sometimes called Care and Repair or Staying Put) that will give specialist advice to older and vulnerable householders and also to people living in private rented accommodation. They are small scale, not-for-profit organisations, usually managed locally by housing associations, councils, or charities. They will usually offer practical help with tasks such as arranging a condition survey, getting estimates from builders (trusted builders) applying for grants or loans and keeping an eye on the progress of work. They may charge a fee towards their assistance, which is usually included in the grant or loans that you may be in receipt of.

To find out whether there is a home improvement agency in your area, you should contact your local Age UK or the local council housing department or Foundations (the National Co-ordinating Body for Home Improvement Agencies) address at the rear of the book.

If there is no Home Improvement Agency in your area you might want to engage a surveyor to carry one out for you. As these are costly, or can be, you should always ask what the cost will be first. The Chartered Surveyor Voluntary Service exists to help people who would other wise be able to get professional advice. You need to be referred to them by a Citizens Advice Bureau first.

Finding a builder

If there is no Home Improvement Agency in your area, you should take care, great care, when trying to find a good reliable builder. We have all heard stories of rogue builders who carry out shoddy work and charge over the odds. If you intend to employ a builder, particularly for a larger job, then you should always employ a builder backed by a proper guarantee scheme. The Federation of Master Builders (FMB) offers a MasterBond Warranty: its members must meet certain criteria and adhere to the FMB's Code of Practice. The ten-year insurance backed warranty will add 1.5% to the total cost of a job but is money well spent. Information on this scheme can be obtained from the FMB website at www.fmb.org.uk. To ensure that you get a good job done, the FMB recommends that you:

- Always ask for references and names of previous clients
- Get estimates from two or three builders
- Ask for the work to be covered by an insurance backed warranty
- Get a written specification and quotation
- Use a contract (the FMB has a plain English contract for small works)
- Agree any staged and final payments before a job
- Avoid dealing in cash.

The FMB has played a leading role in the development of the government backed TrustMark scheme, which is a consumer protection initiative for the home repair and improvement sector. A wide range of traders, including plumbers and electricians, are being licensed to become TrustMark registered firms. For more information contact TrustMark address at the rear of this book.

Financial help with repairs and improvements
Sometimes, individuals find themselves in a position where they cannot afford repairs to their homes. There are, however, various forms of assistance at hand. Local authorities have general powers to provide help with repairs and also adaptations to housing. The assistance isn't always cash based, it can also be provided in the form of labour material or advice. The cash element will usually be either grants or loans. Local authorities will have published policies explaining the various forms of assistance. These can vary from time to time, as many of them

are dependant on national legislation and government funding. Below are a few of the types of grants available.

Disabled facilities grant

These grants provide facilities and adaptations to help a disabled person to live as independently and in as much comfort as possible. They are means tested, i.e., dependant on income, with the exception of grants for disabled children. In its assessment, the council will consider only your income and that of your partner or spouse. The government website www.gov.uk/disabled-facilities-grants outlines all the relevant criteria.

Social services departments provide funding for some minor adaptation works. They may also be able to help with some types of work not covered by the disabled facilities grant.

The Care and Repair England publication also provides useful information about organising and financing building works. You can get a copy by downloading it from the website www.careandrepair.org.

Adapting your home

You may need to make certain adaptations to your home if you or a member of your family needs them, such as mobility aids, to make it easier to navigate the house. There are other areas that can be helpful, such as the positioning of the furniture. Occupational Therapists can give detailed advice. They can assess a person's mobility and their ability to move around and can provide appropriate advice. You should contact your local social services department and ask for an assessment of needs.

You don't have to have a letter from the doctor but this can speed things up. Social services should provide some equipment free if you or a relative is assessed as needing them. All minor adaptations costing less than £1000 must be provided free of charge.

For full information about special equipment and furniture, contact Living Made Easy (formerly the Disabled Living Foundation) www.livingmadeeasy.org.uk at the address at the rear of the book.

/ ****

Ch. 4

Raising Capital from your Home

Equity release schemes

The main principle behind equity release schemes, which enable you to release cash from your home, is that you are offered a lump sum or an income now but you, or your estate, have to pay back a larger sum to compensate the investors (the Equity release companies). This amounts to a longer-term loan which is paid back later with rolled up interest. If you wish to raise money but do not wish to move home then these schemes could be for you. Bear in mind we are in a time of rising interest rates.

Equity release schemes come in two basic forms: lifetime mortgages and home reversion schemes.

Lifetime mortgages

With a lifetime mortgage you borrow against the value of your home but the capital, and usually the interest is repaid only on your death or when you move out. Lifetime mortgages can be taken out jointly with your spouse or partner, in which case the loan does not have to be repaid until the second death. You can use a lifetime mortgage to raise a single large cash sum. If you want an income, you can draw out a series of smaller sums or use a single lump sum to buy an investment, such as an annuity.

The former is more tax efficient because the income from an annuity is usually taxable.

Types of lifetime mortgages

With the most common form of lifetime loan-a roll up loan-interest is added each month to the amount that you owe. You are charged interest not just on the amount that you originally borrowed, but to the increasing balance as interest is added. The interest can be fixed for the whole life of the loan or can be variable. When your home is eventually sold, the proceeds are used to repay the outstanding loan and what is left over goes to your estate. Different providers set different age limits but you must be at least 55 or 60 with most schemes to be eligible for a lifetime mortgage. In addition, the value of your home, less any debts secured against it must be in the region of £50,000 and upwards. If you have an existing mortgage, you will usually be required to pay this off with the loan. The amounts that you can borrow will vary with your age. The maximum for a roll up loan is usually about half the value.

Reversion schemes

With a reversion scheme you sell part, or all, of your home, but retain the right to live there either rent free or for a token rent. When the home is eventually sold, the reversionary company takes a percentage of the sale proceeds, or the whole amount if you sold 100 per cent of your home. This means that the reversion company, as opposed to the estate gets the benefit of any increase in value of your home. A reversion scheme can be taken out singly or jointly, in which case it continues until the second death. As with lifetime mortgages, reversion schemes can pay you a single lump sum or a series of smaller lump sums. Alternatively, they may be combined with an annuity or other investment to provide you with a regular income. Investment income is usually taxable but lump sums from the sale of your home are not. The money that you get when you take out the loan will be smaller than the value of the part of your home that you sell. This difference represents the return to the reversionary company. A key factor that the reversionary company uses in deciding what it will offer is how long it expects to have to wait before it gets its money back. To qualify for a reversionary scheme, you will usually be between 65-70. Your home must be in reasonable condition and worth a minimum amount, typically £75,000.

Alternatives to equity release
One of the most common reasons for considering equity release is to raise extra income for day-to-day living. If this is your main motive, you might want to consider ensuring that the other avenues for raising income have been explored.

For example:
- Are you claiming all the state benefits due to you, such as Pension Credit, Council Tax Benefit and Attendance Allowance
- Have you taken steps to trace any lost pensions that you might be claiming?
- Are you exploiting the potential of your home, for example taking in a lodger?

- Are you making sure that you are not overspending?
- Are you paying too much tax?

You cannot normally use equity release to raise a lump sum of below £10,000. If such a sum is needed you might want to consider taking out an interest only mortgage. Unlike a lifetime mortgage you pay interest each month so the amount borrowed does not grow. The main thing with equity release schemes is that you should get good advice, usually independent advice so that you are totally aware of what it is that you are signing up for. You can contact the Equity Release Council www.equityreleasecouncil.com. All reputable providers of equity release plans are members of this council.

Selling your home

As we all know, the housing market has undergone changes and the value of property, mainly in the Southeast has increased out of all proportion. However, the wisdom of using your home, or factoring in your home, as a source of income when retirement age is reached, is questionable.

Property prices are just one of the problems if your intention is to sell up to release capital for your retirement. The other main one is that if you are aiming to downsize to a smaller home then the price of this property may not necessarily be that much cheaper than the family home that you are selling. This does depend of course on the nature, size and value of that property. In addition, there are also the other problems associated with relocating, such as getting used to a new area, neighbours and so on.

You should bear in mind as well that there are significant costs associated with selling, moving and buying. This will eat into any equity that you release from your property and should be taken into account.

****

Ch. 5

Extras Because of Age

Free bus travel in England for older and disabled people

Eligible older and disabled people are entitled to free off-peak travel on local buses anywhere in England. Off peak is between 9.30am to 11pm Monday to Friday and all-day weekends and public holidays.

The England bus pass only covers travel in England. It doesn't give you free bus travel in Wales, Scotland, or Northern Ireland.

Free bus travel in Wales, Scotland and Northern Ireland

There are similar schemes in each of the above countries and you need to apply to your respective local authorities.

Who is eligible for an older person's bus pass?

If you live in England, you will be entitled to a bus pass when you reach 'eligible age'. If you were born after 5th April 1950, the age you become eligible is tied to the changes in state pension age for women. This affects both men and women.

Women born after 5th April 1950

If you are a woman born after 5th April 1950, you will become eligible for an older person's bus pass when you reach pensionable age.

Men born after 5th April 1950

If you are a man born after 5th April 1950, you will come eligible when you reach the pensionable age of a woman born on the same day. If you were born before 6th April 1950, **y**ou are eligible for an older person's bus pass from your 60th birthday if you were born before 6th April 1950.

Disabled persons bus pass

You are eligible for a disabled person's bus pass if you live in England and are 'eligible disabled'. This means you:

- are blind or partially sighted
- are profoundly or severely deaf
- are without speech
- have a disability, or have suffered an injury, which has a substantial and long term effect on your ability to walk
- don't have arms or have long-term loss of the use of both arms
- have a learning disability.

You are also eligible disabled if your application for a driving licence would be refused under section 92 of the Road Traffic Act 1988 (physical fitness). However, you won't be eligible if you were refused because of persistent misuse of drugs or alcohol.

How to get your bus pass

In the first instance you should contact your local council (whether you live in England, Scotland, Ireland, or Wales, who will tell you who issues passes in your area.

Bus passes in London-the Freedom Pass

If you are eligible disabled or of eligible age and you live in Greater London, you can apply for a Freedom Pass. This gives you free travel on the entire Transport for London network. On most services, you can use the pass at any time. You can also use your Freedom Pass England-wide, but only during off-peak times outside of London. If you wish to use your bus pass on coaches then you should ask the coach company about terms and conditions. For more about bus passes for elderly and disabled go to www.gov.uk/apply-for-elderly-person-bus-pass

Passport

If you were born on or before 2nd September 1929, you no longer have to pay for your passport. You can ask for a refund if you are eligible and have applied for a replacement passport since 19th May 2004.

Health

NHS Prescriptions. Once you reach age 60 you qualify for free NHS prescriptions (Currently £9.65 in 2023/24). If you are eligible, you simply sign the declaration on the back of the prescription. Scotland and Northern Ireland have phased out charges for prescriptions. Prescriptions are already free for all in Wales.

NHS sight tests. From age 60 you also qualify for free NHS sight tests but you still have to pay for the glasses and lenses, unless your income is low. You can get free sight tests from age 40 if you are considered at risk of developing glaucoma because a close family member has this condition (or any age if you already have sight problems).

Help with bills

Winter fuel payments. This scheme is in force all over the UK and provides a cash sum to every household with one or more people over 60 in the 'qualifying week' which is the week beginning the third Monday in September. You can use the cash in any way you like. However, it is designed specifically to help you cope with Winter fuel bills. The standard payment is normally between £100-£300 depending on your situation. If you want more details concerning this payment you should go to www.directgov.co.uk.

Free or discounted Television licence.

You can get either:

- a free TV licence if you're 75 or over and you get Pension Credit
- a discount if you're blind or in residential care.

If you're 75 or over

You can get a free TV licence if you're 75 or older and you either:

- get Pension Credit
- live with your partner who gets Pension Credit

The licence covers everyone living at your address.

You can apply when you're 74 if you already get Pension Credit. You'll still need to pay for your licence until the end of the month before your 75th birthday. After that you'll be covered by your free licence.

How to apply
You can apply for a free licence online.
You can also apply by phone.

TV Licensing
Telephone: 0300 790 6117
Minicom: 0300 709 6050

If you're in residential care
You can get a special licence for £7.50 if you live in an eligible residential care home.

You must be either:
- retired and over 60
- disabled.

Your housing manager can apply for you.

If you're registered blind
You can get a 50% discount if you're registered blind or live with someone who is. The licence must be in the blind person's name - if it's not, you can make a new application to transfer it into their name. You'll need to provide your existing TV licence number when you apply.

Your home

You can get help with heating and fuel efficiency if you are aged 60 or over. You should go to: www.gov.uk/browse/benefits/heating.

Repairs and Improvements

One of the most important elements of your home is that of its condition. When you retire or are close to retiring, this presents the ideal opportunity to assess the overall condition of your home and to draw up a condition survey (or have one drawn up) so that you can plan expenditure. It is wise to commence the work as soon as possible after retirement, or before if possible, so that you can still carry out works yourself, without resorting to using building firms. This will save money and mean that you have more control. This chapter also points the way to the various agencies that exist who will give you advice on repairs and maintenance and funding.

Deciding what needs to be carried out

There are specialist advice agencies, called Home Improvement Agencies (sometimes called Care and Repair or Staying Put) that will give specialist advice to older and vulnerable householders and to people living in private rented accommodation. They are small scale, no-for-profit organisations, usually managed locally by housing associations, councils, or charities. They will usually offer practical help with tasks such as arranging a condition survey, getting estimates from builders (trusted builders) applying for grants or loans and keeping an eye on the progress of work. They may charge a fee towards their assistance, which is usually included in the grant or loans that you may be in receipt of.

To find out whether there is a home improvement agency in your area, you should contact your local Age UK or the local council housing department or Foundations (the National Co-ordinating Body for Home Improvement Agencies). Address at the rear of the book.

If there is no Home Improvement Agency in your area you might want to engage a surveyor to carry one out for you. As these are costly, or can be, you should always ask what the cost will be first. The Chartered Surveyor Voluntary Service exists to help people who would other wise be able to get professional advice. You need to be referred to them by a Citizens Advice Bureau first.

Finding a Builder

If there is no Home Improvement Agency in your area, you should take care, great care, when trying to find a good reliable builder. We have all heard stories of rogue builders who carry out shoddy work and charge over the odds. If you intend to employ a builder, particularly for a larger job, then you should always employ a builder backed by a proper guarantee scheme. The Federation of Master Builders (FMB) offers a MasterBond Warranty: its members must meet certain criteria and adhere to the FMB's Code of Practice. The ten-year insurance backed warranty will add 1.5% to the total cost of a job but is money well spent.

Information on this scheme can be obtained from the FMB website at www.fmb.org.uk. To ensure that you get a good job done, the FMB recommends that you:

- Always ask for references and names of previous clients
- Get estimates from two or three builders
- Ask for the work to be covered by an insurance backed warranty
- Get a written specification and quotation
- Use a contract (the FMB has a plain English contract for small works)
- Agree any staged and final payments before a job
- Avoid dealing in cash.

The FMB has played a leading role in the development of the government backed TrustMark scheme, which is a consumer protection initiative for the home repair and improvement sector.

A wide range of traders, including plumbers and electricians, are being licensed to become TrustMark registered firms. For more information contact TrustMark. Address at the rear of this book.

Financial help with repairs and improvements
Sometimes, individuals find themselves in a position where they cannot afford repairs to their homes. There are, however, various forms of assistance at hand. Local authorities have general powers to provide help with repairs and adaptations to housing. The assistance isn't always cash based, it can also be

provided in the form of labour material or advice. The cash element will usually be either grants or loans. Local authorities will have published policies explaining the various forms of assistance. These can vary from time to time, as many of them are dependant on national legislation and government funding. Below are a few of the types of grants available.

Disabled facilities grant

These grants provide facilities and adaptations to help a disabled person to live as independently and in as much comfort as possible. They are means tested (i.e.) dependant on income, with the exception of grants for disabled children. For more information you should go to www.gov.uk/disabled-facilities-grants

If you receive Pension credit, Income Support or Income based jobseekers allowance, you may be able to get a Community Care Grant or Budgeting Loan from the Social fund to help you with the cost of minor repairs. Social services departments provide funding for some minor adaptation works. They may also be able to help with some types of work not covered by the disabled facilities grant.

If you want to raise capital from your home to pay for works, the Home Improvement Trust may be able to help. It is a not-for-profit company that has links with a number of commercial lenders who provide older people with low-cost loans raised against the value of their home. You can contact Home Improvement Trust direct at the address at the rear of the book.

The Care and Repair England publication also provides useful information about organising and financing building works. You can get a copy by phoning 0115 950 6500 or by downloading it from the website www.careandrepair.org.uk.

Adapting your home

You may need to make certain adaptations to your home if you or a member of your family needs them, such as mobility aids, to make it easier to navigate the house. There are other areas that can be helpful, such as the positioning of the furniture. Occupational Therapists can give detailed advice. They can assess a person's mobility and their ability to move around and can provide appropriate advice. You should contact your local social services department and ask for an assessment of needs. You don't have to have a letter from the doctor but this can speed things up. Social services should provide some equipment free if you or a relative is assessed as needing them. All minor adaptations costing less than £1000 must be provided free of charge.

For full information about special equipment and furniture, contact the Disabled Living Foundation at the address at the rear of the book.

****

Ch. 6

Future Care Options

_____

As is well documented over a third of people over 65-74 and over a half over the age of 75 have a long-standing health condition that affects their lives in some way. The ability to carry on living in one's own home really depends a lot on the availability of appropriate care. Quite often this is not readily available and comes at a cost. Those who are fortunate enough can be cared for by their family.

In 1993, the government introduced policies designed to help more people live independently in their own homes through the expansion of formal support services. This has had the effect of reducing the number of people who need care home support.

However, we are living in an age of an increasing elderly population and there is increased pressure on finances and the ability of government to pay. Whether you are thinking of support in the future for an aging relative or indeed for yourself, there are several main factors that you need to consider and decisions to be made:

- Exactly what form of care might be needed in the future, whether a retirement home or higher-level sheltered housing
- Where will the money come from to pay for the care?

For more information about care homes and costs and fees in Scotland go to:
ttps://www.caresourcer.com/caresupport/financing-care/care-home-fees...
For Northern Ireland go to:
https://www.nidirect.gov.uk/paying-your-residential-care-or...
We need now to examine the various options available.

Care in the home

Most people would rather stay in their own home and receive the appropriate level of support for their needs. Regardless of your own personal financial situation you have the right to approach social services in your local authority area for a needs assessment. Then a manager from the department will visit you in your home (or relative as case may be) and put together a care plan for you.

The whole approach to care in the home and care in residential homes has been redefined by the Care Act 2014, a summary of which is below.

The Care Act 2014

The *Care Act 2014* came into force on 1st April 2015 along with a range of new supporting regulations and a single set of statutory guidance, which, taken together, describe how the Act should be applied in practice. The aim of the change was to simplify and modernize the system, which had become very complex and also to create a new approach to charging. The *Care Act 2014* actually came into force in two stages, in April 2015 and April 2016. Some of the key changes introduced in 2015 were:

- The promotion of individual well being as an overarching principle within all the activities of a local authority including assessment, eligibility, prevention, means testing and care and support planning.

- New national eligibility criterion for both the adult requesting services and their carer(s) leading to rights to services and based around the well-being principle. The previous four local eligibility levels have now become one, set at approximately the previous 'substantial' level. Carers now have an absolute right to have their assessed, eligible, support needs met for the first time; they have a slightly different eligibility criterion to the service user but are subject to the same means test rules.

- A person-centered, outcomes-focused, approach to assessing and meeting needs. Local authorities must consider how to meet each person's specific needs rather than simply considering what existing service they will fit into. They must also consider what someone wants/needs to achieve or do and the effect on them of any difficulties they are having.

- The whole system is now administered via personal budgets and based on the principles of the personalization policy that has been developed over the past few years.

- A 'right to request' service provision for a fee where someone with eligible needs is found to be a self-funder (must pay the whole cost of a service) in the means test. This right does not exist for care home provision.

- New local authority 'market shaping' duties to ensure adequate, diverse, good quality, local service provision.
- The duty to prevent, reduce and delay the need for services and also related duties to integrate care with the NHS where this benefits a service user.
- A lifetime care cost cap above which the State will meet the cost of paying a person's eligible social care needs. The national cap will be reviewed every five years. The announcement by the government to impose a lifetime cap of £86,000 by October 2023 has been delayed till 2025. See below.
- The introduction of care accounts, which will require a local authority to track a person's personal expenditure towards meeting their eligible social care needs, towards the new care cost cap –based on the amount set out in their personal budget. Each account will be adjusted annually in line with the national rise in average earnings. Some local authorities may start to assess care accounts ahead of the April 2016 start date to avoid capacity issues.
- Independent personal budgets for those people with assessed, eligible, needs but who have capital more than the upper threshold and who are meeting the cost of their care and support themselves. This is a choice that will be available to enable payments to be noted in the person's care account.

There are a wide range of support services that can be provided to help you stay in your own home and to assist your carer if you have one. Services could include domiciliary (home) carer and personal assistants; meals delivered at home; day center attendance and respite care; live-in care services; rehabilitation services; sheltered accommodation and supported living; shared lives services; other housing options; community support; counseling; direct payment support organizations; information, brokerage and advice services1.

Other forms of assistance could include the provision of specialist disability equipment, adaptations to your home, community alarms and other types of assistive technology.

For more detailed and specific information about the changes and new criteria introduced in the Care Act you should go to www.ageuk.org.uk they have ready prepared fact sheets which will help you to see what you are entitled to.

There are certain fundamental rules that local authorities must abide by. Charges should not reduce the income that a person has left below a set level. If a person is 60 or over, this is the Pension Credit Guarantee credit level plus a buffer which is dependant where you live in the UK, for example 25% in England and 35% in Wales. The assessment should be based only on your income and generally not that of your partner or anyone else. If you feel that you are paying too much for your care services then you have the right to ask the local authority to review your financial assessment.

Proposed cap on care home fees in England – 2025

- The UK government has announced that from October 2025 (this was originally due to come into effect in 2023 but has been delayed), no one in England will have to pay more than £86,000 in care costs during their lifetime. Once you have reached the cap, the ongoing care costs will be paid for by your local authority.

- The idea behind the cap is that it will put an end to homeowners having to sell their houses to pay for care.
- However, daily living costs at a care home such as accommodation, food and energy bills will not be covered.
- If you have capital between £20,000 and £100,000 you will pay towards your social care costs on a sliding scale.
- Under the plans, if you have less than £20,000, you will not have to pay for care from your assets.

How the care is paid for

Either the local authority will pay you direct in cash for your services or, if you so desire, you can ask the local authority to arrange and pay for the care. The Government has also introduced a scheme called Individual Budgets, arising out of the Care Act 2014, which are similar to Direct Payment, so you receive a cash sum, but it covers a wide range of services so it includes, for example, help towards a warden in sheltered housing. The aim of cash payments is to put the individual in more control of the services that they buy. Obviously, this may not be suited to everyone and some people will be more reliant on the local authority to provide and pay for services.

Other benefits available

There are other benefits available such as personal independence payment (replacing Disability Living allowance for those up to age 64) or if you are over 65 Attendance Allowance. These benefits are tax-free and are not means tested. If you are a carer, you will also have the right to a free needs assessment to pay for extra levels of need.

The care plan devised by the local authority might for example recommend that someone be paid for sitting with a relative whilst you have a few hours off, or respite care (where the disabled person moves temporarily into a care home). You will be expected to pay for these services unless your income and savings are low .

Retirement housing
Retirement housing is known by a number of different names that usually reflects the level of care needed, for example sheltered housing, warden assisted housing or warden-controlled housing. This is designed for people over 60 (sometimes can be 55). Usually, it is a scheme that comprises a number of flats and maybe a few bungalows with communal areas for residents, such as lounge and gardens and in some cases a kitchen for the provision of communal meals. There is also usually a laundry area and an emergency call system plus a warden if included in the overall scheme cost.

Some schemes are private, people buy a lease, known as leasehold schemes for the elderly. Sheltered housing to rent is normally provided by local authorities and, more usually now, housing associations. To qualify for these schemes, you have to prove that you are in need and cannot afford to buy. You may qualify for Housing Benefit.

The main cost associated with retirement housing, whether rented or owned, is the service charge. As an ex-care home manager myself, I have long experience of the difficulties that surround service charges.

The service charge covers the cost of wardens, communal areas, emergency call system and gardening. Many other areas are included. If you are on a low income then you might be eligible for housing benefit for some of the services.

Ordinary sheltered housing does not include care services, this has to be arranged with your local authority. However, as discussed, sheltered housing can be more intensive and the levels of charges will reflect this. For example, do you, or a relative envisage needing intensive care of a kind provided by category one sheltered housing or will you need a lesser degree of care?

Moving to a care home

If you move to a care home to receive personal care you may have to pay some or all of the fees yourself, depending on your income. If your main aim is health care, the NHS should pay. This is called NHS continuing care. In some circumstances, you may receive care at home either to avoid admission to hospital or to enable you to leave hospital early.

In this case, you are entitled to free care-called intermediate care-which may include a mix of health and social care. The social care element should be free for a maximum of six weeks.

If your primary reason for moving to a care home is for help with personal care such as getting up, going to bed, bathing and so on, in general you are expected to pay for the fees yourself unless your income and savings are low. In that case, the local authority will carry out a financial assessment to determine whether you should pay anything at all. This assessment is in line with the capital limits which can be obtained from your local authority.

Even if your main need is personal care, you may require some nursing care as well and this is provided free, up to set limits depending where you live in the UK and, in England, on the extent of the nursing care that you need. The Government pays these sums direct to your care provider. If you are paying for your care home fees yourself, you are likely to qualify for Attendance Allowance. If the NHS or local authority is paying for some or all the fees, you will not be able to get Attendance Allowance as well.

As described above, the Care Act 2014 has affected the way in which home care and care home funding is allocated and you should contact Age UK to find out more.

Assessing your finances
Whether or not you can get state funding depends in part on how much capital you have (means testing). Capital includes savings and investments but can also include your house. However, if you're partner (married or not), an elderly or disabled relative or a child under 16 still lives there, the value of your home is disregarded.

The local authority also has the discretion to ignore your home, if, for example, your carer will carry on living there.

How will my capital be treated in the means test?

Your capital is the phrase used to describe the total amount of your savings, any property you own and any shares you might have. It does not include your pension and benefits you might be getting. There are also some national differences. In Wales for example, there's a cap on the maximum you'll have to pay. While in Scotland, care services are free up to a specified limit. The Age UK website gives a full breakdown of fees payable in the UK. Briefly, in 2023 these are:

- If you live in England and have assets (this includes property, savings and investment) of more than £23,250, you will have to pay the full cost of your care and are referred to as a self-funder.
- In Scotland, the threshold for paying for care home accommodation is £32,750. In Scotland if you are eligible for personal care, this will be paid for by your local council.
- In Wales, the care and care home fees threshold is £50,000.
- In Northern Ireland, the threshold for care and care home fees is the same as England, £23,250.
- Anyone with capital below these amounts will qualify for some financial support. In England and Northern Ireland if you have capital below £14,250 you should get maximum support.
- In Scotland, you need to have capital below £20,250 to be eligible for maximum support.
- In Wales, anyone with capital under £50,000 will receive fully funded care from the local authority.

If you are a couple, the local authority is not allowed to base the financial assessment on your joint resources. It must consider only the capital and income that belongs to you. If you are holding assets on behalf of someone else you must prove that they are not your assets or the local authority will treat them as your assets. You can be treated as still owning capital if you are deemed to have deliberately deprived yourself of it. This could be the case if you have given away assets to other family members in advance of applying for a care assessment. Spouses and civil partners are in law liable to support each other and can be asked to contribute towards fees, but the local authority should not do this if it would cause financial hardship. The local authority cannot ask an unmarried partner or other family member to contribute.

How much will I have to pay?

After the means test the local authority should give you a written record of their decision of what you will have to pay and what they will pay, and how they calculated it. You should not be left with less than £28.25 (2023/2024) a week after any contribution to your fees. This is known as your Personal Expenses Allowance. The full PEA for the UK is:

- England: £28.25
- Scotland : £32.65
- Wales: £33.99 (in Wales it's called Minimum Income Amount) (applies to tax year 2023/24)
- Northern Ireland: £27.19

The allowance is for personal items such as stationery, birthday cards and toiletries. This amount will not be taken into account by the local authority when it is calculating how much you should contribute towards your care. English local authorities have the discretionary power to increase the personal expenses allowance in special circumstances such as if the resident has property-related expenses or is supporting a spouse.

What if I run out of money?

If you are paying fees yourself (called self-funding) and your capital goes down to less than £23,250, the local authority may assist with funding. You should request an assessment a few months before that happens. They should arrange one as soon as possible so you don't have to use up your capital below that amount.

Planning ahead for care

If you think that you will need care for a long time, taking out a long-term care product could work out cheaper than the fees. Planning ahead is very difficult and there is no real way to know what your needs will be. There are a few providers of long-term care products and these tend to be expensive. One obvious route is to take out some form of insurance. In the UK, there is just one provider of long-term care insurance. It targets healthy individuals aged 50-70 years. With high premiums (for example around £100 per month for a policy that would pay out a flat rate of £1000 a month it is easy to see why the take up of this insurance is limited.

A handful of providers offer what is known as impaired life annuities that you buy at the point when you need care. You pay a lump sum and in return get an income that pays all or a substantial part of your care costs. The income is tax-free provided that it is paid direct to the provider. The amount that you pay for the annuity will depend on the monthly payments that you need and also the annuity providers assessment of how long that it will have to pay out.

****

Ch. 7

Income Tax Generally-How it affects You

_____

Income Tax

Regardless of whether we are employed, retired or self-employed, we all have to accept the fact that HMRC are going to take a percentage of our income in the form of income tax and there is nothing we can do to avoid it.

The retired, employed and self-employed are treated in slightly different ways and therefore we shall look at each individually, once we have assessed the structure of income tax. You should check your current tax allowances with HM Revenue and Customs as they are subject to annual change. For more information about tax and state and other pensions see chapter 9 onwards

Personal allowance

Most people are allowed to receive a certain amount of income before tax is payable. This is known as the basic personal allowance. In 2023/2024 allowances are:

Band	Taxable income	Tax rate
Personal Allowance	Up to £12,570	0%
Basic rate	£12,571 to £50,270	20%
Higher rate	£50,271 to £125,140	40%

Band	Taxable income	Tax rate
Additional rate	over £125,140	45%

You don't get a Personal Allowance on taxable income over £125,140.

Income above £100,000

If your income is above £100,000, the basic personal allowance is further reduced by £1 for each £2 earned over the £100,000 limit, irrespective of age.

Blind person's allowance

You may also be entitled to an additional allowance if you or your spouse or registered civil partner are blind or have severely impaired sight. This is another full relief allowance as it is treated in the same way as the personal allowance, so increases the amount of income you can receive before you start to pay tax. In 2023-24 this allowance is £2,870.

In England and Wales

If you live in England or Wales, you will need to be certified as blind and appear on a local authority register of blind people to claim this allowance.

In Scotland and Northern Ireland

If you have not been certified as blind and live in Scotland or Northern Ireland, you will qualify for the allowance if your eyesight is so bad that you are unable to perform any work where your eyesight is essential.

Unused balance

If your income is not enough to make use of the allowance, any unused balance can be transferred to your spouse or registered civil partner. Married couples get certain tax breaks.

Married couple's allowance

You only qualify for this allowance if you or your husband, wife or registered civil partner were born before 6 April 1935. Unlike the personal allowance, the married couple's allowance is not an amount you can earn before you start paying tax. Instead, it's a restricted relief allowance, which means the tax you pay is reduced by deducting 10% of the allowance from your final tax bill.

Marriage transferable tax allowance

Additionally, from April 2023, married couples born after 1935 will be able to transfer up to £1,260 of unused personal allowance (Marriage transferable tax allowance).

Claiming maintenance relief

You can claim this relief for certain maintenance payments you make if you or your ex-spouse or registered civil partner were born before 6 April 1935 and you pay the maintenance under a legally binding agreement. It works in a similar way to the married couple's allowance.

Your tax bill will be reduced by 10% of the maintenance relief allowance or the amount you pay in maintenance if that amount is lower.

The Employed

If you are employed your tax affairs are conducted on the fiscal year or financial year which is 6th April to 5th April the following year. You are taxed on what is known as Schedule E (Pay As You Earn) which means that both tax and national insurance will be deducted by your employer before you receive your salary. You therefore receive your salary net of tax. This is without doubt the simplest way to conduct your tax affairs as there is very little further communication you need to have, if any, with your tax office.

At the end of the financial year, you will receive a P60 which is a statement of your full year's earnings and it will contain details of how much tax and national insurance you have paid as well as pension contributions if you are in an occupational pension scheme.

You should always keep your P60 in a safe place as it often requested by banks and building societies for mortgage or loan purposes.

If you work for a large employer, you may receive fringe benefits such as a company car, mortgage subsidy, or private medical insurance. These are very worthwhile benefits but you must remember they are also taxable benefits which will mean that your personal allowance will reduce to account for the real value of these benefits. If you have such benefits but notice your tax code hasn't changed then it is your responsibility to inform your tax office, as failure to do so may mean that in future years they could claim payment for undisclosed benefits.

Not all benefits are taxable, however, and the most attractive one is obviously a company pension scheme. In recent years a great deal of companies have moved towards Performance Related Pay. When you leave employment, you will be provided with a P45 which is similar to a P60 but is for the benefit of your new employer to use in order to calculate your earnings to date and therefore make the necessary stoppages in your salary. It is always worthwhile taking a copy of your P45 for your own reference.

The self-employed

If you are self employed your own tax year can be any period of 12 months you want. In the eyes of the Inland Revenue, you will be taxed on what is known as Schedule D and pay Class 2 National Insurance contributions. Being self employed means that the money you receive for the services you provide will be gross and therefore no tax will have been deducted.

It is advisable that you keep an accurate record of all the money you receive and receipts for any money you spend in connection with your business activities. At the beginning of April, you would normally receive a tax return form which explores all the potential sources of income you may have. This must be duly signed and returned within a month.

A large percentage of the self employed use the services of an accountant, as they best know the ways in which your tax liability can be reduced and their services certainly make it easier if you are self-employed and are hoping to take out a mortgage.

HM Revenue and Customs will negotiate with you or your accountant once they have details of your year's earnings and business expenses. Once the expenses have been taken from the gross figure this will leave your net income and therefore the amount upon which you will be expected to pay tax. Your tax liability is normally paid in 2 instalments, the first on 1st January and the second on the 1st of July. The Inland Revenue, however, do not wait for your accounts to be completed and in most cases, you will be expected to make instalments based on assessments of your expected income and once your accounts are finalised you will then be informed of any over or under payment.

Tax and pensions
You pay tax if your total annual income adds up to more than your Personal Allowance. Your total income could include:

- the State Pension you get (either the basic State Pension or the new State Pension)
- Additional State Pension
- a private pension (workplace or personal) - you can take some of this tax-free
- earnings from employment or self-employment
- any taxable benefits you get
- any other income, such as money from investments, property or savings.

You may have to pay Income Tax at a higher rate if you take a large amount from a private pension. You may also owe extra tax at the end of the tax year.

Lifetime allowance
You usually pay a tax charge if the total value of your private pensions is more than £1,073,100 (Lifetime allowance). Your

pension provider will take off the charge before you get your payment.

Tax if someone inherits your pension

Other rules apply if someone inherits your State pension or your private pension. You won't usually pay any tax if your total annual income adds up to less than your Personal Allowance.

Lump sums from your pension

You can usually take up to 25% of the amount built up in any pension as a tax-free lump sum. The tax-free lump sum doesn't affect your Personal Allowance. Tax is taken off the remaining amount before you get it.

Example:

Your whole pension is worth £60,000. You take £15,000 tax-free. Your pension provider takes tax off the remaining £45,000. When you can take your pension depends on your pension's rules. It's usually 55 at the earliest. You might have to pay Income Tax at a higher rate if you take a large amount from your pension. You could also owe extra tax at the end of the tax year.

How you can take your pension
A pension worth up to £10,000

You can usually take any pension worth up to £10,000 in one go. This is called a 'small pot' lump sum. If you take this option, 25% is tax-free.

You can usually get:

- up to 3 small pot lump sums from different personal pensions
- unlimited small pot lump sums from different workplace pensions

A pension worth up to £30,000 that includes a defined benefit pension

If you have £30,000 or less in all your private pensions, you can usually take everything you have in your defined benefit pension as a 'trivial commutation' lump sum. If you take this option, 25% is tax-free. If this lump sum is paid from more than one pension, you must:

- have your savings in each scheme valued by the provider on the same day, no more than 3 months before you get the first payment
- get all payments within 12 months of the first payment.

If you take payments from a pension before taking the rest as a lump sum, you pay tax on the whole lump sum.

Cash from a defined contribution pension

Check with your provider about how you can take money from a defined contribution pension. You can take:

- all the money built up in your pension as cash - up to 25% is tax-free.
- smaller cash sums from your pension - up to 25% of each sum is tax-free.

You may have to pay a tax charge on money you put into your pension after you withdraw cash.

If your life expectancy is less than a year

You may be able to take all the money in your pension as a tax-free lump sum, if all of the following apply:

- you're expected to live less than a year because of serious illness
- you're under 75
- you don't have more than the lifetime allowance of £1 million in pension savings.

If you're over 75 you'll pay Income Tax on the lump sum. Check with your pension provider. Some pension funds will keep at least 50% of your pension for your spouse or civil partner.

Capital Gains Tax

If you have successfully bought and sold investments, antiques and property etc., you may find that you would be liable for capital gains tax. Everyone is allowed to make a profit on opportunities that they fund with their own capital. There is, however, a limit, which you should check with HMRC, and any profit/gain that exceeds that figure would be liable for capital gains tax at the individual's marginal rate.

Tax on dividends

You may get a dividend payment if you own shares in a company. In April 2023/24, the first £1,000 is tax free.

Above this allowance the tax you pay depends on which Income Tax band you're in. Add your income from dividends to your other taxable income when working this out. You may pay tax at more than one rate.

Tax band	Tax rate on dividends over £1,000
Basic rate	8.5%
Higher rate	32.75%
Additional rate	39.35%

Inheritance Tax

The subject of death is one which is rarely discussed openly and inheritance tax is thought to be an issue that is largely limited to the wealthy. This, however, is a misconception, as inheritance tax will affect more people now than ever before. In order to establish whether you are going to have an inheritance tax bill, you must assess the total value of the estate left by the deceased. This would include all assets and any gifts made within the preceding seven years. If the total figure exceeds £325.000 (2023-24) there will be a liability on the surplus of 40%. If the estate totals less than £325,000 there will be no liability. You should check these limits with HMRC as they are subject to change. It now becomes clear that if you have been able to build a reasonable amount of savings, paid off your mortgage and may have received a pension lump sum and an inheritance yourself, you could be bordering on the £325,000 limit and your estate would be liable for inheritance tax. You should not restrict your own lifestyle to reduce your beneficiaries' tax bill but if you can afford it there are various options and exemptions that could substantially reduce the future liability.

Exemptions

1. There is no inheritance tax between husband and wife.

2. To a U.K charity.

3. Gifts that total £3,000 a year.

4. £250 gifts made to anyone and however many people you like. This cannot be given to the same people as the £3,000.

5. Wedding presents, £5,000 from a parent, £2,500 from a grandparent, £1,000 from friend or family.

6. Part of a divorce settlement.

7. To support female parent-in-law if she is divorced, widowed, or separated.

8. Selected agricultural land or business assets and unquoted shares.

Gifts made seven years before death

Any gifts that the deceased made in the last 7 years of his or her life will be liable to inheritance tax on a sliding scale and the value of the gift will also form part of the estate. In order to reduce the liability, you could write any life insurance policies you have under trust and should you die, the benefits of your policies would not form part of your estate, but be payable to your spouse or children, therefore avoiding possible inheritance tax. For more detailed advice on taxation, you should go to the HMRC website at www. hmrc.gov.uk

****

Ch. 8

Making a Will

It is often said that the toughest job in sales is to get people to buy fire extinguishers: no one wants to think that they and their family could be caught in a fire which could kill or injure. The same thinking seems to apply to making a will: most people in Britain have not made a will- something which their families could well come to regret.

There are two sorts of people for whom making a will is not just a good idea, but essential: Anyone who is reasonably well off or whose affairs are at all complicated, and anyone who is in a partnership. Unmarried partners (or outside a civil arrangement) cannot inherit from each other unless there is a will: your partner could end up with nothing when you die, unless they can show that they were financially dependent.

There is no such thing in England as a 'common-law marriage.'

The State moves in

- When anyone dies without making a will, the law, i.e. the state, takes over. In the extreme case, where you die single and have no other surviving relatives, all your estate could end up with the Crown. And the law is not at all generous to your spouse: if you have no children If there are no surviving children, grandchildren or great-grandchildren, the partner will inherit:

* all the personal property and belongings of the person who has died and
* the whole of the estate with interest from the date of death.

If there are children, the widow/widower will get £270,000, plus personal assets and income from 50% of the rest; the children will get 50% when they reach age 18 and the other 50% when the surviving parents die. If you aim to save inheritance tax, you need to make a will. For 2023-24 the 'nil rate band' is fixed at £325,000 which means that no tax is due below that level, and anything more is taxed at 40%.

How to make a will

So how do you make a will? You can draw up your own using a will-making kit which you can buy from a big stationer or download from the net. That represents the most cost-effective choice and it could work if your affairs are reasonably straightforward. But if you think that your will could be disputed, i.e., subject to legal challenge, then you need to go to a solicitor. That will be a few hundred pounds well spent and you may qualify for legal aid on financial grounds or because of age: you could ask Citizens Advice. You will probably know a solicitor or have employed one in a recent property deal. You will talk to friends, or you can contact the Law Society for a list of solicitors near where you live.

Put yourself on paper

Before you go to your solicitor, there are two important things you need to do. Firstly, you need to put yourself on paper - everything you own that is of significant size, including cars, jewelry, property, home contents, bank accounts, shares and life insurance. At the same time, you put down all that you owe, such as mortgage, overdraft and credit card debts. You need to give precise details of the beneficiaries and be very specific about what you are leaving them.

The second thing you need to do is choose an executor, one or two people whose job is to ensure that your wishes are carried out. Your first thought may be someone younger than you (you will need their agreement to act) but there is no guarantee that they will outlive you. If no executor has been designated, the state will appoint a solicitor for you - for a fee. If you go to a solicitor, think about a formula, e.g. a partner appointed by whoever is senior partner of the firm at the time. The executors will need to know where your will is kept, with your solicitor or in your bank.

Time to revisit?

You have made your will, but you should resolve to look at it again, say every five years: people change, as do assets and liabilities. It is a good basic rule to revisit your will when a new child arrives or when you move house. Outside events can change a will: if you were single when you drew up your will, it may become invalid if you get married. But divorce or separation do not make a will invalid, so you might want to make changes. If you just want to make minor alterations, you can add supplementary changes known as codicils. These are added separately and all alterations have to be properly witnessed. If the alterations are significant, you will need to make a new will which will revoke any other wills you have made.

The case for making a will is essentially simple: as Benjamin Franklin said, death and taxes are certain, and making a will means that your family will not have to spend time and energy sorting out a complicated financial and legal set-up. But when you look beyond middle age you have to assess probabilities - you may be out of the country when your signature is needed, you may get ill, or you may be injured. We are now talking power of attorney.

Power of attorney

You probably gave your solicitor a power of attorney when you sold your flat; you may have given a power of attorney to your partner when you had to go on an overseas business trip but wanted to buy some shares in the UK. The power of attorney simply gives a person the power to act for somebody else in their financial affairs or in health and personal welfare. (Rules in Scotland are different). The power of attorney you gave your solicitor was probably an ordinary power of attorney, created for a set period and for a specific piece of business. That all seems very practical, you may think, but why should you give anyone a power of attorney? The short answer is that if you are away or fall ill, you will need someone to look after your affairs - and that requires power of attorney. (If this happens and you had not given a power of attorney, your friends and relatives would have to go to court, which would take time and cost money)

Ending the power

When you have given a power of attorney, there are two ways in which it can be ended. You can end it yourself by using a deed of revocation or it will end automatically if you, the donor, lose 'mental capacity.' This is where problems can arise. Suppose you gave your partner an ordinary power of attorney to handle your bank account while you go on your overseas business trip; you are mugged while on your trip and lie unconscious in hospital. Your power of attorney is ended because you are mentally out of action; for the same reason you cannot give a new power of attorney. Your partner cannot legally access your bank account or have any involvement in your affairs: catch 22? The answer to this puzzle was to create an Enduring Power of Attorney. Under an EPA when you were mugged on your overseas trip, your partner and/or solicitor would register with the court and they could then act on your behalf. New EPAs cannot be created since October 2007.

New lasting powers

EPA's have been replaced by Lasting Powers of Attorney which have separate sections for personal welfare and for property and affairs. Each of these must be registered separately and the LP A can only be used - similar to an EPA - once it has been registered with the

Office of the Public Guardian. If you want to change your mind, you can cancel all the different Powers of Attorney, so long as you are still mentally capable. This may all sound elaborate but it represents the only answer to the situation where you cannot manage your affairs because of accident, illness, age or whatever - but someone needs to do so.

The need for a power of attorney is now that much greater because banks and financial institutions are more aware of their legal responsibilities. Formerly, a friendly bank manager might have been prepared to help your partner sort out what needed to be done while you were out of action. Now, your friendly bank manager is more likely to stick to the legal rules, if only to protect himself and his employer.

You as attorney

One of your colleagues may ask you to be his attorney; if you agree, make sure that a firm of solicitors are also involved. You will have some costs - such as when you register the power of attorney - and there are strict rules, for keeping money and property separate and for keeping accounts of any dealings for the person who gave you the power. When you register, you are obliged to tell your colleague's relatives who are free to object. This is not a job for a layman acting all by himself.

****

Ch. 9

Pensions and Planning for the Future

Planning for the future

The main principle with all pension provision is that the sooner you start saving money in a pension plan the more you will have at retirement. The later that you leave it the less you will have or the more expensive that it will be to create a fund adequate enough for your needs. The following chapters outline pensions and sources of pensions in detail. It may be that, if you are already retired you cannot take advantage of certain pension schemes, such as occupational pensions. However, if you are looking at your various options before retirement then the information should prove useful.

In order to gauge your retirement needs, you will need to have a clear idea of your lifestyle, or potential lifestyle in retirement. This is not something that you can plan, or want to plan, at a younger age but the main factor is that the more that you have the easier life will be. There are two main factors which currently underpin retirement:

* Improved health and longevity-we are living longer and we have better health so therefore we are more active
* People are better off-improved state and company pensions.

93

Sources of pension and other retirement income

Government statistics indicate that there is a huge gap between the poorest and richest pensioners in the United Kingdom. No surprise there. The difference between the richest fifth of single pensioners and the poorest fifth is about £400 per week. The poorest fifth of pensioners in the UK are reliant mainly on state benefits whilst the wealthier groups have occupational incomes and also personal investment incomes. The outline below indicates sources of pension and the disparity between the richest and poorest socio-economic groups:

The Pensioners Income Series

The Pensioners' Incomes (PI) Series contains estimates of the levels, sources and distribution of pensioners' incomes. It also examines the position of pensioners within the income distribution of the population as a whole. The latest figures are for 2021/22. More updated information appears periodically and can be found at: www.gov.uk/government/collections/pensioners-incomes-series.

Average income of pensioners

The figures show that the median weekly income for single pensioners is £285 (2021/22), down from £312 in the 2012-13 tax year. Income earned by retired workers is made up of several sources including the state pension, workplace pensions, personal pensions and income from savings and investments.

Pensioners need £33,000 for a comfortable retirement moneyfacts.co.uk In order for workers to enjoy a comfortable retirement that includes holidays abroad, a generous clothing allowance and a car they will need to have saved enough for a £33,000 per year income.

Couples tend to have more retirement income than single people. Some reports even suggest that in 2017/18, retired couples received more than twice the income of single retirees. This may partly be due to the fact that housing costs were included in the study – couples sharing housing will generally have lower overheads than someone on their own. Another factor may be that those who are single upon entering retirement are likely to be divorced or separated, which may have had a significant impact on their past finances and thus their ability to save for retirement. People in long-term stable relationships may have a greater capacity for building up retirement funds, as well as a stronger motivation for doing so.

Sources of pensioner incomes

Nearly all pensioners (97 per cent) were in receipt of the State Pension in 2021/22. Income-related benefits were received by a quarter of all pensioners in 2019/20. The percentage of pensioners in receipt of income-related benefits has decreased from 34 per cent in 2005/06 to 25 per cent in 2021/22. This has been influenced by the increase in the State Pension and the targeting of Pension Credit on the pensioners on lowest incomes. There has been little change in the percentage of pensioners with income from disability benefits. This income category covers a range of benefits paid to individuals as a result of their disability status.

Personal pensions provide income to a smaller group of pensioners than occupational pensions. The percentage of pensioners in receipt has increased over a 10-year period. In 2021/22, 18 per cent of pensioners were in receipt of income from personal pensions, compared with 12 per cent in 2005/06. Recently retired pensioners were more likely to be in receipt than older pensioners, which reflects the relatively recent expansion in the numbers contributing to personal pensions. Personal pensions in their current form were introduced in 1988.

Private pension income includes all non-State Pension income. Over the past 10 years, there has been an increase in the percentage of pensioners receiving income from private pensions – from 66 per cent to 70 per cent. Investment income was the third most common source of income, received by 63 per cent of all pensioners in 2021/22 although the percentage of pensioners in receipt of investment income has decreased from 70 per cent over the past 10 years. Overall, 17 per cent of pensioners were in receipt of earnings. Some of the results for pensioner couples include earnings from one person being under State Pension age.

Pensioners income according to position-bottom fifth of pensioners and top fifth
Benefit income, including State Pension income, was the largest source of income for both single pensioners and couples in the

bottom fifth of the income distribution. For pensioner couples in this group benefit income accounted for 78 per cent of their income, while for single pensioners this was 86 per cent. Benefit income made up more than half of all income for all but the top fifth of single pensioners.

For the top fifth of both couples and singles, the largest source of income was from private pension income (38 per cent for couples and 44 per cent for singles). For couples the proportion of income from earnings was highest in the top fifth of the income distribution.

Amongst other things, the above illustrates that those in the poorest and wealthiest bands have a wide gap in income, in particular in the areas of earnings and investments. The richest have managed to ensure that there is enough money in the pot to cater for retirement. Those in the lower income bands rely heavily on state pensions and other benefits. The Pensioners Income Series measures those within the bottom, middle and top fifth of the population.

How Much Income is needed in Retirement-Planning Ahead
When attempting to forecast for future pension needs, there are a number of factors which need to be taken into account:

These are:
- Your income needs in retirement and how much of that income you can expect to derive from state pensions

- How much pension that any savings you have will produce
- How long you have to save for
- Projected inflation.

Income needs in retirement

This is very much a personal decision and will be influenced by a number of factors, such as ongoing housing costs, care costs, projected lifestyle etc. The main factor is that you have enough to live on comfortably. In retirement you will probably take more holidays and want to enjoy your free time. This costs money so your future planning should take into account all your projected needs and costs. When calculating future needs, all sources of income should be taken into account.

What period to save over

The obvious fact is that the longer period that you save over the more you will build up and hence the more that you will have in retirement. As time goes on savings are compounded and the value of the pot goes up. One thing is for certain and that is if you leave it too late then you will have to put away a large slice of your income to produce a decent pension. If you plan to retire at an early age then you will need to save more to produce the same benefits.

Inflation

As prices rise, so your money buys you less. This is the main effect of inflation and to maintain the same level of spending power you will need to save more as time goes on. Many forms of retirement plans will include a calculation for inflation. Currently, inflation is at a very high level, around 10% with food inflation running even higher. Interest rates are high, to combat inflation, which is a bonus for savers and those with annuities.

History shows that the effects of inflation can be corrosive, having risen above 25% per annum in the past.

For most people, retirement is a substantial part of life, probably lasting a couple of decades or more. It follows that ensuring your financial security in retirement requires some forward planning. Developing a plan calls for a general review of your current finances and careful consideration of how you can build up your savings to generate the retirement income that you need.

There are five distinct stages to planning your retirement which are summarised below.

Stage 1-this involves checking first that other aspects of your basic finances are in good shape. Planning for retirement generally means locking away your money for a long time. Once invested it is usually impossible to get pension savings back early, even in an emergency. It is therefore essential that you have other more accessible savings available for emergencies and that you do not have any problem debts that could tip you into a financial crisis. You must then weigh up saving for retirement against other goals that are more pressing, such as making sure that your household would be financially secure if you were unable to work because of illness or the main breadwinner dies.

Stage 2-You need to decide how much income you might need when you retire. There is a table overleaf which might help you in calculating this.

Stage 3- Check how much pension that you have built up so far.

Stage 4-Compare your amount from stage 3 with your target income from stage 2.

Stage 5-Review your progress once a year and/or if your circumstances change.

It is a fact that many people need far less in retirement than when actively working. The expenses that exist when working, such as mortgage payments, children and work-related expenses do not exist when retired. The average household between 30-49 spends £473 per week and £416 between 50-64. This drops to £263 per week between 65 to 74 and even lower in later retirement (Expenditure and Food Survey).

However, as might be expected, expenditure on health care increases correspondingly with age. Whilst the state may help with some costs the individual still has to bear a high proportion of expenditure on health-related items. When calculating how much money you will need in retirement, it is useful to use a table in order to list your anticipated expenses as follows.

(See overleaf)

Everyday needs

Item	Annual Total
Food and other	
Leisure (newspapers etc)	
Pets	
Clothes	
Other household items	
Gardening	
General expenses	

Home expenses

Mortgage/rent	
Service charges/repairs	
Insurance	
Council tax	
Water and other utilities	
Telephone	
TV licence other charges (satellite)	
Other expenses (home help)	

Leisure and general entertainment

Hobbies	
Eating out	
Cinema/theatre	
Holidays	

Other luxuries (smoking/drinking	

Transport

Car expenses	
Car hire	
Petrol etc	
Bus/train fares	

Health

Dental charges	
Optical expenses	
Medical insurance	
Care insurance	
Other health related expenses	

Anniversaries/birthdays etc

Children/grandchildren	
Relatives other than children	
Christmas	
Charitable donations	
Other expenses	

Savings and loans

General savings	
Saving for later retirement	
Other savings	
Loan repayments	

Other

The above should give you an idea of the amounts that you will need per annum to live well. Obviously, you should plan for a monthly income that will meet those needs. You should also take account of income tax on your retirement incomes.

****

Chapter 10

Sources of Pensions-A Summary

For certain, one area that people should be thinking about as they approach retirement is the amount of income they will need to live on and what they will get. The state pension is a reliable source of income. However, it is almost certain that a person will need more than this.

The state pension

Over 96% of single pensioners and 99% of couples receive the basic state pension. Therefore, it is here to stay. Everyone who has paid the appropriate national insurance contributions will be entitled to a state pension. If you are not working you can either receive pension credits, as discussed, or make voluntary contributions.

The full (basic) state pension is £156.20 for a single person (2023) From April 2023, for men who were born after 6th April 1951 and women who were born after 6th April 1953 the pension is £203.85 per week. This is known as a 'flat rate' or 'single tier' system and is designed to make the current system more simple and easier to understand. Getting the flat rate, however, is very much dependant on contributions.

Basic state pensions are increased each April in line with price inflation. State pensioners also receive a (£10 Christmas bonus-check current entitlement) and are entitled to winter fuel payments. Married women can claim a pension based on their spouse's NI record. Men who have reached 65 are also able to claim a basic state pension based on their wife's contribution record where the wife reaches state pension age on or after 6th April 2010.

Same sex couples, as a result of the Civil Partnerships Act 2004, along with married couples of the same sex, following the passing of the Marriage (Same sex Couples Act) 2014, have the same rights as heterosexual couples in all aspects of pension provision.

Transsexual people

Your State Pension might be affected if you're a transsexual person and you:

- were born between 24 December 1919 and 3 April 1945
- were claiming State Pension before 4 April 2005
- can provide evidence that your gender reassignment surgery took place before 4 April 2005

You don't need to do anything if you legally changed your gender and started claiming State Pension on or after 4 April - you'll already be claiming based on your legal gender. For more details go to www.gov.uk/state-pension/eligibility

How many qualifying years to get the full State Pension?

The number of qualifying years you need to get a full state pension depends on when you reach your State Pension age. If you reach State Pension age on or after 6 April 2010 but before April 2016, you need 30 qualifying years. If you reach State

Pension age on or after 6 April 2016, you normally need 35 qualifying years.

Using someone else's contribution record

In some circumstances, you may be able to use your husband's, wife's or civil partner's contribution record to help you qualify for a State Pension.

Pension credits

Pension credits began life in October 2003. The credit is designed to top up the resources of pensioners whose income is low. The pension credit has two components: a guarantee credit and a saving credit.

The guarantee credit

This is available to anyone over a qualifying age (equal to women's state pension age-see further on) whose income is less than a set amount called the minimum guarantee. The guarantee will bring income up to £201.05 for a single person and £306.85 for a couple (including civil partners and same sex couples) (2023-2024). The minimum guarantee is higher for certain categories of disabled people and carers. The qualifying ge or Pension Credit is gradually going up to 66 in line with the ncrease in the State Pension age for women to 65 and the urther ncrease to 66 for men and women.

The savings credit

You can only claim savings credit if you or your partner are aged 65 or over. It's intended as a modest "reward" if you've provided yourself with a retirement income over and above the basic retirement pension. Savings credit is calculated by the The maximum savings credit you can get is £15.94 a week if you're single and £17.84 a week if you're married or living with a partner.

The income taken into account for savings credit is the same as for guarantee credit, but various types of income are now ignored. These are Working Tax Credit, contribution-based Employment and Support Allowance, Incapacity Benefit, contribution-based Jobseeker's Allowance, Severe Disablement Allowance, Maternity Allowance and maintenance payments made to you (child maintenance is always ignored).

If your income is still over the savings threshold, the Pension Service works out your entitlement to savings credit.

If you reach State Pension age on or after 6 April 2016

Most people who reach State Pension age on or after 6 April 2016 won't be eligible for Savings Credit. But you may continue to get Savings Credit if both of the following apply:

- you're in a couple and one of you reached State Pension age before 6 April 2016
- you were getting Savings Credit up to 6 April 2016
- If you stop being eligible for Savings Credit for any reason from 6 April 2016, you won't be able to get it again.

National Insurance Credits

In some situations, you may get National Insurance Credits, which plug what would otherwise be gaps in your NI record. You might get credits in the following situations:

- when you are unemployed, or unable to work because you are ill, and claiming certain benefits
- If you were aged 16 to 18 before 6 April 2010, you were usually credited automatically with National Insurance credits. No new awards will be made from 6 April 2010.
- if you are on an approved training course
- when you are doing jury service
- if you are getting Statutory Adoption Pay, Statutory Maternity Pay, Additional Statutory Paternity Pay, Statutory Sick Pay, Maternity Allowance or Working Tax Credit
- if you have been wrongly put in prison
- if you are caring for a child or for someone who is sick or disabled
- if you are aged 16 or over and provided care for a child under 12, that you are related to and you lived in the UK for the period(s) of care
- if your spouse or civil partner is a member of Her Majesty's forces and you are accompanying them on an assignment outside the UK.

There are special arrangements for people who worked or were detained without pay in Iraq during the Gulf Crisis. If you think you might be affected by this, write to HM Revenue & Customs (HMRC) at: HM Revenue & Customs
National Insurance Contributions & Employer Office
Benton Park View, Newcastle upon Tyne
NE98 1ZZ
Tel: 0300 200 3211

The State Pension age

Currently, the state pension age is 66 for men and women. There will be further increases in the state pension age to 68 for men and women. The increase in the State Pension age is being phased in and your own pension age depends on when you were born. The proposed changes affect people born between April 1953 and 5th April 1960. (For your own retirement age you should go to the Pensions Service Website).

Additional state pension

S2P replaced the State Earnings Related Pension (SERPS) in April 2002. SERPS was, essentially, a state second tier pension and it was compulsory to pay into this in order to supplement the basic state pension. There were drawbacks however, and many people fell through the net so S2P was introduced to allow other groups to contribute. S2P refined SERPS allowing the following to contribute:

- People caring for children under six and entitled to child benefit
- Carers looking after someone who is elderly or disabled, if they are entitled to carers allowance
- Certain people who are unable to work because of illness or disability, if they are entitled to long-term incapacity benefit or severe disablement allowance and they have been in the workforce for at least one-tenth of their working life
- Self-employed people are excluded from S2P as are employees earning less than the lower earnings limit. Married women and widows paying class 1 contributions at the reduced rate do not build up additional state pension.

S2P is an earnings-related scheme. This means that people on high earnings build up more pension than those on lower earnings. However, people earning at least the lower earnings limit are treated as if they have earnings at that level and so build up more pension than they otherwise would.

Contracting out

A person does not build up state additional pension during periods when they are contracted out. Contracting out means that a person has opted to join an occupational scheme or a personal pensions scheme or stakeholder pension. While contacted out, a person will pay lower National Insurance Contributions on part of earnings or some of the contributions paid by an employee and employer are 'rebated' and paid into the occupational pension scheme or other pension scheme.

Increasing your state pension

There are a number of ways in which you can increase your State Pension, particularly if you have been presented with a pension forecast which shows lack of contributions and a diminished state pension. You can fill gaps in your pension contributions or you can defer your state pension. HM Revenue and Customs have a help line on 0300 200 3300 to check your record and to receive advice on whether you have gaps and how to fill them.

Filling gaps in your record

If you wish to plug gaps in your contributions, normally you can go back 6 years to fill gaps in your record. However, if you will reached State Pension Age before April 5th, 2015, special rules let you fill any gaps up to six years in total going back as far as 6th April 1975. You can make class 3 contributions to fill the gap, each contribution costs £17.45 (2023/4) so a full year's worth costs 52 times £17.45 = £907.40). Making class three contributions can't increase your additional state pension. However, Class 3 contributions do count towards the state bereavement benefits that your wife, husband or civil partner could claim if you were to die.

Deferring your state pension
Another way to boost your state pension is to delay its commencement. You can put off drawing your pension for as long as you like, there is no time limit. You must defer your whole pension, including any additional or graduated pensions and you earn an addition to the lump sum or a bigger cash sum.

In the past, if you put off drawing your own pension and your wife was getting a pension based on your NI record, her pension would also have to be deferred and she would have to agree to this. From 6th April 2010 onwards, husbands and civil partners as well as wives may be able to claim a pension based on their partners' record. But a change to the rules now means that, if you defer your pension and your wife, husband, or civil partner claims on your record, they no longer have to defer their pension as well. If your pension has already started to be paid, you can decide to stop payments in order to earn extra pension or lump sum. But you can only defer your pension once. You can earn an increase in the pension when it does start of 1% for every five weeks you put off the pension. This is equivalent to an increase of 10.4% for each whole year.

Alternatively, if you put off claiming your pension for at least a whole year, you can earn a one-off lump sum instead of extra pension. The lump sum is taxable but only at the top rate you were paying before getting the lump sum. Whatever the size of the sum it does not mean that you move tax brackets. The Pension Service, which is part of the Department of Work and Pensions publishes a detailed guide to deferring your state pension. Go to www. gov.uk-contact-pension-service.

Women and Pensions

It is a general rule that women pensioners tend to have less income than their male counterparts. Therefore, when building a retirement plan, women need to consider what steps they and their partners can take to make their financial future more secure.

Particular issues for women

These days, the rules of any pension scheme-whether state or private, do not discriminate between men and women. Whether male or female you pay the same to access the same level of benefits. However, this does not always mean that women end up with the same level of pension as men. This is because of the general working and lifestyle differences between men and women, for example women are more likely to take breaks from work and take part time work so they can look after family. As a result, women are more likely to pay less into a pension fund than men.

Historically, the (idealised) role of women as carers was built into the UK pensions system. Not least the state pension system. It was assumed that women would marry before having children and rely on their husbands to provide for them financially right through to retirement. As a result, women who have already retired typically have much lower incomes than men. Changes to the state scheme for people reaching state pension age from 6th April 2010 onwards, mean that most women will, in future, retire with similar state pensions as men. However, if you are an unmarried women living with a partner you should be aware of the following:

The state scheme recognises wives, husbands and civil partners but not unmarried partners. This means that if your unmarried partner dies before you, you would not be eligible for the state benefits that provide support for bereaved dependants.

Occupational schemes and personal pensions typically pay survivor benefits to a bereaved partner, whether married or not. However, many schemes-especially in the public sector-have recognised unmarried partners only recently and, as a result, the survivor pension for an unmarried partner may be very low.

The legal system recognises that wives, husbands and civil partners may have a claim on retirement savings built up by the other party in the event of divorce, but these will be considered along with all the other assets to be split between you and you may end up with a much lower retirement income than you had been expecting.

The legal system does not give similar rights to unmarried partners who split up. If your unmarried partner was building up pension savings for you both, he or she can walk away with all those savings and you have no legal claim on them.

Effects of changes to the state pension from 2016 on women

As we have discussed, from April 2023, the new "flat rate " state pension will typically be £203.85 a week, but only for those who have paid national insurance contributions (NIC's) for 35 years. Many women will not qualify, having taken career breaks to care for children.

If there are gaps in your entitlement then consider buying some added years of state pension which you can do in the run-up to retirement. The state pension purchase scheme is far more generous than any private pension, provided you live more than a few years in retirement. Be careful, though, that you're not going to be buying years that you'd actually make up through work between now and retirement, otherwise you could end up giving the government money for something you'd have got anyway. Voluntary NIC's cost £3.45 a week for Class 2 and £17.45 a week for Class 3 (2023/4) and you can normally fill gaps from the past six years. If you are due to retire after April 2016, check to see how much you will receive at gov.uk/future-pension-centre.

Have you told the government you are a carer?

The good news is that full-time unpaid carers will be entitled to the same pension as those who have worked in a paid full-time job from 2016. However, thousands of women who do not claim child benefit or carers' allowance could miss out.

These benefits signal to the Department for Work and Pensions (DWP) that an individual qualifies for NIC's. Since households earning above £50,000 are no longer eligible to claim full child benefit, and those earning over £60,000 will receive no child benefit at all, many stay-at home mums may go under the radar. Similarly, if women are caring for a family member but not claiming carer's allowance their unpaid work will go unrecognised. If you are a carer but don't claim any benefits pro-actively contact the DWP to report your situation.

If your household income is over £50,000 but under £60,000 you should still register for child benefit in order to receive NIC's.

The over 80 pension

This is a non-contributory pension for people aged 80 or over with little or no state pension. If you are 80 or over, not getting or getting a reduced state pension because you have not paid enough National Insurance contributions (NI) and are currently living in England, Scotland or Wales and have been doing so for a total of 10 years or more in any continuous period of 20 years before or after your 80th birthday, you could claim the over 80 pension. The maximum amount of the over 80 state pension that you can get is currently £93.60 per week (2023/24).

Occupational pensions

Briefly, occupational pension schemes are a very important source of income. With Occupational pension schemes the contract is between the company and the pension provider. With Group Personal Pension Schemes, which we will also be discussing later, although the employer chooses the company the contract is between the employee and the pension company.

Occupational pension Schemes are one of the best ways to pay into a pension scheme as the employer must contribute a significant amount to the pot. Over the years the amounts paid into occupational pension schemes has increased significantly. Although there have been a number of incidences of occupational schemes being wound up this is relatively small and they remain a key source of retirement income.

From October 2012, it has been compulsory for employers to provide an occupational pension scheme, Auto Enrolment. For the first time, employers are obliged to:

- enrol most of their workforce into a pension scheme; and
- make employer pension contributions.

Stakeholder schemes

Stakeholder pension schemes are designed for those people who do not have an employer or had an employer who did not have an occupational scheme. They therefore cannot pay into an occupational scheme. If an employer did not offer an occupational scheme (many small employers were exempt) they had to arrange access to a stakeholder scheme. Employees did not have to join an occupational scheme offered by employers, instead they could join a stakeholder scheme. Likewise, self-employed people can also join a stakeholder scheme.

Stakeholder schemes have a contribution limit-this being currently £3,600 per year. Anyone who is not earning can also pay into a scheme, up to the limit above. You pay money to a pension provider (e.g., an insurance company, bank or building society) who invests it (e.g., in shares). These are a type of personal pension, but they must meet some minimum standards set by the government. These include:

- management charges can't be more than 1.5% of the fund's value for the first 10 years and 1% after that
- you must be able to start and stop payments when you want or switch providers without being charged
- they must meet certain security standards, e.g., have independent trustees and auditors.

How much can be invested in a stakeholder pension?

There is no limit to the amount that can be invested in a stakeholder pension scheme. However, tax relief can only be obtained on contributions up to a maximum annual contribution limit (known as an individual's 'annual allowance'). For the tax year 2024/24, this is set at the lower of 100% of an individual's UK earnings or £60,000 per annum. Carry forward of unused allowances may be permitted in some circumstances. It is possible to contribute up to £4,000 per year (including tax relief) into a stakeholder pension scheme even if a person is not earning. A member of an occupational pension scheme may also contribute to a stakeholder pension scheme. You can start making payments into a stakeholder pension from £20 per month. You can pay weekly or monthly. If you don't want to make regular payments, you can pay lump sums any time you want.

The rules for stakeholder pensions changed on 1 October 2012. If you're starting a new job now or returning to one, your employer doesn't have to offer you access to a stakeholder pension scheme. They now have to offer entry through automatic enrolment. If you're in a stakeholder pension scheme that was arranged by your employer before 1 October 2012, they must continue to take and pay contributions from your wages. This arrangement is in place until:

- you ask them to stop
- you stop paying contributions at regular intervals
- you leave your job
- If you leave your job or change to another personal pension, the money they have paid in stays in your pension pot unless you have it transferred to a different pension provider.

Other ways to save for retirement

The government offers certain tax advantages to encourage pension saving. However, the most advantageous savings plan is the Individual Savings Account (ISA) discussed previously. In addition, you might have regular savings accounts, your home or a second home. All these possibilities must be factored in when arriving at an adequate retirement income.

****

Chapter 11

Private Pension Savings Generally

The lifetime allowance

There is a single lifetime limit on the amount of savings that a person can build up through various pension schemes and plans that are subject to tax relief. (This excludes the state pension). The lifetime allowance is £1,073,100m from April 2023.

The lifetime allowance applies to savings in all types of pension schemes including occupational pensions and stakeholder schemes. There are, broadly, two types of scheme or plan:

- Defined contribution-with these types of schemes money goes in and is invested with the fund used to buy a pension. Basically, if the fund at retirement is £200,000 then £200,000 lifetime allowance has been used up.

- Defined benefit-in this type of scheme, a person is promised a pension of a certain amount usually worked out on the basis of salary before retirement and the length of time that you have been in the scheme. The equation for working out lifetime benefit in this type of scheme is a little more complicated. The pension is first converted into a notional sum (the amount of money it is reckoned is needed to buy a pension of that size). The government sets out a factor that it says will be needed to make the conversion which it has said is 20. If the pension is £20,000 then this is calculated as £20,000 times £20,000 which is £400,000. Therefore £400,000 will be used up from the lifetime allowance.

Protecting the Lifetime Allowance

The standard lifetime allowance is £1,073,100 on 6 April 2023. But you may be able to protect your pension savings from the annual reductions. These reductions can be complicated and to get full details you should go to:

https://www.gov.uk/guidance/pension-schemes-protect-your-lifetime-allowance

The annual allowance

The annual allowance (amount that an individual can contribute to a pension) is £60,000 (April 2023). This is the amount that pension savings may increase each year whether through contributions paid in or to promised benefits. In addition, you can carry forward unused allowances from three years previously the annual allowance will not start in the year a person starts their pension or die. This gives a person scope to make large last-minute additions to their fund. If at retirement the value of a pension exceeds the lifetime allowance there will be an income tax charge of 55% on the excess if it is taken as a lump sum, or 25% if it is left in the scheme to be taken as a pension, which is taxable as income. If the increase in the value of savings in any year exceeds the annual allowance, the excess is taxed at 40%.

Limits to benefits and contributions

The present benefit and contribution limits have been scrapped. The only remaining restrictions are:

- Contributions-the maximum that can be paid in each year is either the amount equal to taxable earnings or £3,600 whichever is the greater
- Tax free lump sum-at retirement a person can take up to one quarter of the value of the total pension fund as a tax-free lump sum

Taking a pension

Savings do not have to be converted into pension in one go. This can be staggered and pension income can be increased as a person winds down from work.

For each tranche of pension started before 75, there is a range of choices. This will depend on the rules of each individual scheme. A person can:

- Have a pension paid direct from an occupational pension scheme
- Use a pension fund to purchase an annuity to provide a pension for the rest of life
- Use part of the pension to buy a limited period annuity lasting just five years leaving the rest invested
- Opt for income drawdown which allows taking of a pension whilst leaving the rest invested. The tax-free lump sum could be taken and the rest left invested. The maximum income will be 120% of a standard annuity rate published by the Financial Conduct Authority. On death

the remaining pension fund can be used to provide pensions for dependants or paid to survivors as a lump sum, taxed at 35%.

From 6 April 2015, where the member dies before the age of 75, spouses or other beneficiaries who inherit joint life or guaranteed term annuities will no longer be taxed on the income. This aligns their treatment with dependant drawdown pensions.

It was also confirmed that drawdown pensions paid to spouses, or other dependants or nominees, would be tax-free where the member died before reaching the age of 75 and the pension first comes into payment on or after 6 April 2015. The fund can also be passed on tax-free as a lump sum, rather than potentially being subject to a 55% charge.

Not all dependant pensions will benefit from the tax exemption, however. Where the member dies before the age of 75 with either uncrystallised funds or a drawdown fund, if the beneficiary chooses to buy an annuity with the fund rather than go into drawdown, this will remain fully taxable. Similarly, there is no provision for making inherited scheme pensions (e.g., widow's pensions from final salary schemes) tax-free. Where the member dies after reaching the age of 75, all dependant pensions remain taxable, as they are under the current rules. Dependants who are already in receipt of annuities before 6 April 2015 will remain taxed on them in the same way as dependant drawdown pensions.

When a person reaches 75 years of age, they must opt for one of the following choices:

- Have a pension paid direct from an occupational scheme
- Use the pension fund to buy an annuity to provide a pension for the rest of life or
- Opt for an Alternatively Secured Pension or ASP. This is pension draw down but with the maximum income limited to 90% of the annuity rate for a 75-year-old. On death, the remaining fund can be used to provide dependants pensions or, if there are no dependants, left to a charity or absorbed into the scheme to help other people's pensions. The person(s) whose pensions are to be enhanced can be nominated by the person whose pension it is.

We will be discussing options for taking pensions in more depth in Chapter 15

****

Chapter 12

Choosing a Personal Pension Plan

There is a wide choice of personal pension schemes on offer. One common denominator is that the schemes are now heavily regulated by both the government and the Financial Conduct Authority. Most schemes will accept either a monthly contribution or a one-off lump sum payment per annum. The majority of schemes will allow a person to increase contributions. It is important to look for a plan that will allow a person to miss payments, in case of unemployment, sickness etc, without penalty.

Investments

Plans which allow individuals to choose their own investments are called' Self-invested Personal Pensions' (SIIPS) (see below). A person will build up their own fund of personal investments from a wide range of options such as shares, gilts, property and other areas. However, unless an individual has a large sum to invest, this is unlikely to be a wise bet. Pension companies can offer their own expertise and usually have far greater knowledge than the individual.

Self-invested Personal Pensions (SIPPs)

A self-invested personal pension (SIPP) is a pension 'wrapper' that holds investments until you retire and start to draw a retirement income. It is a type of personal pension and works in a similar way to a standard personal pension. The main difference is that with a SIPP, you have more flexibility with the investments you can choose.

How it works

SIPPs aren't for everyone. Get advice if you're thinking about this type of personal pension. With standard personal pension schemes, your investments are managed for you within the pooled fund you have chosen. SIPPs are a form of personal pension that give you the freedom to choose and manage your own investments. Another option is to pay an authorised investment manager to make the decisions for you.

SIPPs are designed for people who want to manage their own fund by dealing with, and switching, their investments when they want to. SIPPs can also have higher charges than other personal pensions or stakeholder pensions. For these reasons, SIPPs tend to be more suitable for large funds and for people who are experienced in investing.

What you can and can't invest in

Most SIPPs allow you to select from a range of assets, such as:

- Unit trusts.
- Investment trusts.
- Government securities.
- Insurance company funds.
- Traded endowment policies.
- Some National Savings and Investment products.
- Deposit accounts with banks and building societies.

- Commercial property (such as offices, shops or factory premises). Individual stocks and shares quoted on a recognised UK or overseas stock exchange.

These aren't all the investment options that are available – different SIPP providers offer different investment options. It's unlikely that you'll be able to invest directly in residential property within a SIPP. Residential property can't be held directly in a SIPP with the tax advantages that usually accompany pension investments. But, subject to some restrictions, including on personal use, residential property can be held in a SIPP through certain types of collective investments, such as real estate investment trusts, without losing the tax advantages.

How you access money in your SIPP
New rules introduced in April 2015 mean you can access and use your pension pot in any way you wish from age 55, (However, see below 'accessing your pension funds to finance your business').

There's a lot to weigh up when working out which option or combination will provide you and any dependants with a reliable and tax-efficient income throughout your retirement. Be sure to use the free, government-backed Pension Wise service to help you understand your options or get financial advice.

As mentioned, you should note that in 2019, the **Money and Pensions Service** replaced Pension Wise, The Money Advice Service and the Pensions Advisory Service, which will all be under the new umbrella. For further information about the timing of this go to their website: www.moneyandpensionsservice.org.uk

Small Self-Administered Schemes (Ssas)

A SSAS is essentially an employer sponsored pension scheme with fewer than 12 people, where at least one member is connected with another, or with a trustee or the sponsoring employer, and where some or all the scheme assets are invested other than in insurance policies.

Every registered pension scheme is required to have a Scheme Administrator. If a Scheme Administrator is not appointed, then the Scheme trustees will normally become the Scheme Administrator by default. The Scheme Administrator must enrol online with HMRC before they can register the SSAS. Contributions to the SSAS must not be paid by either the employer or a member until the scheme has been registered with HM Revenue and Customs.

Any contributions, even if they are only paid to the Trustees' bank account before the scheme is registered will not receive tax relief. The managing trustees must open a Scheme bank account. Contributions from the company (and the members) are paid into the bank account before they are invested at the managing trustees' discretion (subject to certain restrictions).

The structure of a Small Self-Administered Scheme could, for example, be as follows:

- Company and member payments
- Trustees' bank account
- Insurance Company investments

Self-administered part
– Commercial property e.g., company premises.
– Loans to employer.
–Deposit accounts.
– Open Ended Investment Companies (OEICs).
– Stock Exchange
– e.g., equities.
– Securities, etc
– e.g., gilts.
– Trustee Investment Bond.

There are clear benefits to holding assets under a registered pension scheme. For example, no capital gains tax liability arises when scheme assets are sold. On the other hand, when personally held assets are sold this can trigger a Capital Gains Tax liability.

An SSAS:

- Gives the managing trustees wide investment powers.
- Is a possible source of loan capital to the company for business expansion purposes, which may help minimise reliance on a third party (eg. bank).
- May be able to buy the company's premises – the SSAS managing trustees act as the landlord, meaning that the members retain control.
- Can be a possible source of equity capital for business expansion purposes which could avoid partial surrender of control to external interests.
- Is a vehicle for the managing trustees to back their investment judgement. A SSAS generally appeals to

controlling directors who want To retain control over their pension benefits.

- To use the self-investment facility to help the company's development.
- A greater say in the way pension payments are invested.

Releasing funds to finance business

One of the important points here is that, if the scheme is a small, self-administered scheme it can be accessed to provide funds for a business, even if you are under the age of 55. This is known as 'pension-led funding'. Both SIIP's and SSAS's serve as an appropriate vehicle for this.

To effect pension-led funding you set up a sale and leaseback type arrangement whereby your pension buys assets from your business or loans money to your business secured against your retirement funds. However, it should be noted that there are advantages and disadvantages of doing this so you would need to talk the matter through with a pension provider with knowledge of this area. Scottish Widows is one such provider. There are many more. A reputable financial advisor will be able to point you in the right direction.

Fees and other charges

Those who invest your money on your behalf don't work for nothing. Fees are charged. The rate of interest offered will reflect the ultimate charge and there will probably be an administration fee too. Some plans have very complicated charging structures and it is very important that these are understood before decisions are made.

Other benefits from a personal pension

A personal pension scheme does not automatically offer a package of benefits in addition to the actual pension. Any additional benefits must be paid for. The range of extra benefits includes lump sum life cover for dependants if death occurs before retirement, a pension for widow or widower or other partner, a waiver of contributions if there is an inability to work and a pension paid early if sickness or disability prevents working until retirement age.

A contracted out personal pension must allow for a widow's or widower's pension to be payable if the widow or widower is over 45 years of age, or is younger than 45 but qualifies for child benefit. The pension would be whatever amount can be bought by the fund built up through investing the contracting-out rebates. The widow or widower has an open market option, which gives him or her a right to shop around for a different pension provider rather than remain with the existing provider.

The pension could cease if the widow or widower remarries while under the state pension age or ceases to be eligible for child benefit whilst still under 45. This depends on the terms of the contract at the time of death.

A contracted-out widows or widower's pension built up before 6th April 1997 must be increased each year in line with inflation, up to a maximum of 3% a year. For post April 1997 pensions this must be up to 5% per year and after 6th April 2005, pensions taken out don't have to increase at all.

With the exception of contracted out plans, a person must choose at the time of taking out the plan which death benefits to have as part of the scheme. Broadly, they should be in line with the benefits mentioned above.

Retirement due to ill health

If a person must retire due to ill health, a pension can be taken from a personal plan at any age. However, a person's inability to work must be clearly demonstrated and backed up with a professional opinion.

Taking a pension early will result in a reduced pension because what is in the pot will be less. However, there are ways of mitigating this, one way to ensure that a waiver of premiums in the event of sickness is included in the pension. In this way the plan will continue to grow even though a person is ill. Another way is to take out permanent disability insurance. This insurance will guarantee that the pension that you will get when you cannot work will at least be a minimum amount.

The Pension Protection Fund

Members of defined benefit occupational pension schemes are protected through the PPF, which will pay regular compensation, based on your pension amount, if the company becomes insolvent and the pension scheme doesn't have enough money to pay your pension. The PPF applies to most defined benefit schemes where the employer became insolvent after 6th April 2005. You should check with the PPF about levels of compensation.

The Financial Assistance Scheme

If you are an individual scheme member and have lost out on your pension as a result of your scheme winding up after 1st January 1997 and the introduction of PPF, you may be able to get financial help from the FAS, which is administered by The Pension Protection Fund, if:

- your defined benefit scheme was under funded and
- your employer is insolvent, no longer exists or has entered into a valid compromise agreement with the trustees of the pension fund to avoid insolvency; or
- in some circumstances, your final salary scheme was wound up because it could not pay members benefits even if the employer continues trading.

In the case of fraud or theft

If the shortfall in your company pension scheme was due to Fraud or theft, it may be possible to recover some of the money through the PPF who operate what is known as the Fraud Compensation Scheme.

The Pension Tracing Service

If you think that you may have an old pension but are not sure of the details, the Pension Tracing Service, part of the Pension Service, may be able to help. They can be contacted on 0800 122 3170 (general enquiries) and will give you full details of their scheme and also will tell you what they need from you in order to trace the pension. www.pensiontracingservice.com.

****

Chapter 13

Pensions and Benefits for Dependants

State pensions

If you die before your spouse or civil partner has reached state pension age, there may be some entitlement to state bereavement benefits if you have built up the appropriate NI contributions in the years prior to your death. The following bereavement payment system is now in place in 2023:

- You may be able to get Bereavement Support Payment if your partner has died. It has replaced the following benefits:
- Widowed Parent's Allowance - if you already get this, your payments will continue until you're no longer eligible
- Bereavement Allowance (previously Widow's Pension)
- Bereavement Payment
- This guide is also available in Welsh (Cymraeg).

Eligibility

Bereavement Support Payment is not means-tested. This means what you earn or how much you have in savings will not affect what you get.

It's usually paid as a one-off payment followed by up to 18 monthly payments. This may change depending on when you make your claim.

When your partner died, you must have been:

- under State Pension age
- living in the UK or a country that pays bereavement benefits
- Your partner must have either:
- paid National Insurance contributions for at least 25 weeks in one tax year since 6 April 1975
- died because of an accident at work or a disease caused by work
- You cannot claim Bereavement Support Payment if you're in prison.

Your relationship to your partner

When your partner died you must have been either:

- married or in a registered civil partnership
- living together as though you were married.

If you were married or in a registered civil partnership with the person who died

You could claim Bereavement Support Payment if your partner died in the last 21 months but you might get less than the usual 18 monthly payments. You must claim within 3 months of your partner's death to get the full amount. You may still be able to claim Bereavement Support Payment if your partner's cause of death was confirmed more than 21 months after the death. Call the Bereavement Service helpline. If your partner died before 6 April 2017, you may be able to get Widowed Parent's Allowance instead.

If you were living together as though you were married with the person who died
You may be able to get Bereavement Support Payment if your partner died on or after 6 April 2017.

You must have been:

- under State Pension age when your partner died
- under State Pension age on 30 August 2018
- If you reach State Pension age within 18 months of your partner's death, you can make a claim but you might get fewer monthly payments.
- When your partner died, you must have been one of the following:
- getting Child Benefit
- eligible for Child Benefit
- pregnant

If you do not get Child Benefit, you must make a new claim for it in your name before you can apply for Bereavement Support Payment. If your partner was getting Child Benefit, you will not automatically get Bereavement Support Payment. You'll need to make a new claim for it in your name before you apply for Bereavement Support Payment. If your partner died before 6 April 2017, you may be able to get Widowed Parent's Allowance instead. The amount of Bereavement Support Payment you can get will depend on your relationship to the person who died and when you make your claim.

If you were married or in a registered civil partnership with the person who died

You'll get the higher rate if one of the following applied when your partner died:

- you were getting Child Benefit
- you were eligible for Child Benefit
- you were pregnant
- This is made up of:
- a first payment of £3,500
- up to 18 monthly payments of £350
- If you were not eligible for Child Benefit, you'll get the lower rate unless you were pregnant when your partner died.
- This is made up of:
- a first payment of £2,500
- up to 18 monthly payments of £100

You must claim within 12 months of your partner's death to get the first payment. If you claim after this time, you will only get monthly payments.

If you were living together as though you were married with the person who died
If your partner died before 30 August 2018
You will not get a first payment and may get up to 18 monthly payments of £350. You must make your claim before 9 February 2024 to get any monthly payments.

If your partner died on or after 30 August 2018, but before 9 February 2023

You may get a first payment of £3,500 and up to 18 monthly payments of £350. You must make your claim before 9 February 2024 to get the full amount.

If your partner died on or after 9 February 2023

You may get a first payment of £3,500 and up to 18 monthly payments of £350. To get the first payment of £3,500, you must claim within 12 months of your partner's death. To get all of the monthly payments, you must claim within 3 months of your partner's death.

When you reach State Pension age and make a claim

If you reach State Pension age within 18 months of your partner's death, you may get fewer monthly payments.

If you get benefits

Bereavement Support Payment will not affect your benefits for a year after your first payment. After a year, the money you have left from your first payment could affect the amount you get if you renew or make a claim for another benefit. You must tell your benefits office (for example, your local Jobcentre Plus) when you start getting Bereavement Support Payment.

Death after retirement

If you die after you and your spouse/civil partner have both reached State Pension age help is given through the State pension system. Your spouse or partner, if they do not receive a full basic pension in their own right, may be able to make up the pension to the full single person's rate, currently £203.85 per week (2023/24 new rate) by using your contribution record. In addition, they can inherit half of any additional State Pension you had built up. To find out more about bereavement benefits contact your local jobcentre plus if you are of working age at www.direct.gov.uk. Advice on a full range of bereavement benefits for those who are retired can also be obtained here.

Occupational and personal schemes

Occupational and personal schemes may also offer pensions and lump sum pay-outs for your survivors when you die. Schemes can pay pensions to your dependants (but not anyone who was not dependant or co-dependant on you) whether you die before or after you started your pension. This means your husband, wife, civil partner, children under the age of 23 or, if older, dependant on you because of physical or mental impairment.

Also, anyone else financially dependant on you can benefit. Under the tax rules, all the dependents' pensions added together must not come to more than the retirement pension you would have been entitled to, but otherwise there is no limit on the amount of any one pension, although individual scheme rules may set some limits.

Dependant's pensions from salary-related schemes

Subject to tax rules governing such schemes, a scheme can set its own rules about how much pension it will provide for dependants. Typically, a scheme will provide a pension for a widow, widower, civil partner or unmarried partner on:

- death before you have started your pension
- death after you have started your pension.
- This will typically be half or two thirds of the pension that you were entitled to at the time of your death. The pension must be increased in line with inflation. If you have been contracted out through a salary related pension scheme before April 1977, the scheme must pay a guaranteed minimum pension (GMP) to the person entitled equal to half the GMP's you had built up.

Lump sum death benefits

The options available to your beneficiaries after you die will depend on how you choose to take your pension and at what age you die. In the event of your death whilst in drawdown your beneficiaries will have the following options under the current rules:

- **Take the pension as a lump sum** Any beneficiary can inherit some or all of your remaining fund. They can do what they like with it. This payment will be tax free if you die before reaching age 75 or taxed at the beneficiary's marginal rate of income tax if after.
- **Continue with drawdown** A dependant or nominated beneficiary can continue to receive your fund as drawdown. Income from which will be tax free if you die before reaching age 75 or taxed at the beneficiary's marginal rate of income tax if after.
- **Convert the drawdown fund to a lifetime annuity** A dependant or nominated beneficiary can use your remaining drawdown fund to purchase a lifetime annuity.

The income will be tax free if you die before reaching age 75 or taxed at the beneficiary's marginal rate of income tax if after.

Pensions are typically held in trust outside your estate and so in most cases are free of inheritance tax (IHT). Death benefits set up more than two years after death may lose their tax-free status. If you make a pension contribution or reduce the income you are drawing from your drawdown plan while in ill health or within two years of death the funds may still be liable to IHT. Tax charges may also apply if you exceed the lifetime allowance and die before age 75.

This information is based on 6 April 2023 pension rules and is subject to change. Tax rules & benefits can change and their value will depend on your personal circumstances.

****

Chapter 14

Pensions-Options for Retirement and Tax Implications for Private Pensions

---

Retirement options and taxation of pensions

As you will know by now, changes introduced from April 2015 give you freedom over how you can access your pension savings if you're 55 or over and have a pension based on how much has been paid into your pot (such as a defined contribution, money purchase or cash balance scheme).

Options for using your pension pot

Depending on your age and personal circumstances some or all the options outlined below could be suitable for you. Your main options are:

1. Keep your pension savings where they are and take them later on in life.

2. Use your pension pot to get a guaranteed income for life – called a Lifetime annuity. The income is taxable, but you can choose to take up to 25% of your pot as a one-off tax-free lump sum at the outset.

3. Use your pension pot to provide a Flexible retirement income, take 25% of your pension pot (or 25% of the amount you allocate for this option) as a tax-free lump sum, then use the rest to provide a regular taxable income.

4. Take a number of lump sums – the first 25% of each cash withdrawal from your pot will be tax-free. The rest will be taxed.

5. Take your pension pot in one go – the first 25% will be tax-free and the rest is taxable (up t0 £268,275) in 2023.

6. Mix your options – choose any combination of the above, using different parts of your pot or separate pots.

We will now look at each of these six options, and the implications, in turn.

1. Keep your pension savings where they are

With this option, your pot continues to grow tax-free until you need it – potentially providing more income once you start taking money out. You (and your employer) can continue making contributions however there are restrictions on how much you can save each year and over a lifetime and still receive tax relief.

In most cases you can get tax relief on pension contributions, including any employer contributions, on the lower of 100% of your earnings or up to £60,000 each year (2023-24 tax year) until age 75. However, if you are a high earner the limit on how much tax-free money you can build up in your pension in any one year depends on your 'adjusted income'. If you don't pay Income Tax, you can still get tax relief on up to £3,600 of pension savings each year until age 75.

However, you will need to check with your pension scheme or provider whether there are any restrictions or charges for changing your retirement date, and the process and deadline for telling them. You need to know whether there are any costs for leaving your pot where it is – some providers charge an administration fee for continuing to manage your pension. Check that you won't lose any valuable income guarantees – for example, a guaranteed annuity rate – if you delay your retirement date.

One other important point is that the money you have saved into your pension pot could continue to grow, but it could also go down in value, as with any investment. Remember to review where your pot is invested as you get closer to the time you want to retire and arrange to move it to less risky funds if necessary.

If you want your pot to remain invested after the age of 75, you'll need to check that your pension scheme or provider will allow this. If not, you may need to transfer to another scheme or provider who will. Not all pension schemes and providers will allow you to delay. If you want to delay but don't have this option, shop around before moving your pension.

On death, any unused pension pots normally fall outside your estate for Inheritance Tax purposes and can be passed on to any nominated beneficiary. In both cases the money continues to grow tax-free while still invested.

If you die before age 75: Provided the beneficiary takes the money within two years of the provider being notified of the pension holder's death, they can take it as a tax-free lump sum or as tax-free income. If they take it later (whether as a lump sum or income) it will be added to their other income and taxed at the appropriate Income Tax rate.

If you die age 75 or over: When the money is taken out (lump sum or income) it will be added to the beneficiary's income and taxed at the appropriate Income Tax rate. However, if the beneficiary is not an individual but is, for example, a company or trust, any lump sum will be taxed at 45%.

2. Use your pension pot to get a guaranteed income for life

A guaranteed income for life – known as a lifetime annuity – provides you with a guarantee that the money will last as long as you live. Guaranteed lifetime income products include basic lifetime annuities; Investment-linked annuities.

The options

You can choose to take up to 25% (a quarter) of your pot as a one-off tax-free lump sum at the outset Up to £268,275. You use the rest to buy a guaranteed lifetime income – a lifetime annuity – from your provider or another insurance company. You must buy within six months of taking your tax-free lump sum. As a rule of thumb, the older you are when you take out a guaranteed lifetime income product, the higher the income you'll get. You can choose to receive your income monthly, quarterly, half-yearly or yearly, depending on the scheme or provider. This type of income is taxable.

Basic lifetime annuities

Basic lifetime annuities offer a range of income options designed to match different personal circumstances. You need to decide whether you want:

- one that provides a guaranteed income for you only and stops when you die –a single life annuity, or one that also provides an income for life for a dependant or other nominated beneficiary after you die – a joint life annuity (normally provides a lower regular income as it's designed to pay out for longer)

- payments to continue to a nominated beneficiary for a set number of years (for example 10 years) from the time the guaranteed income starts, in case you die unexpectedly early – called a guarantee period (can be combined with a single or joint life annuity). For example, if you opt for a guarantee period of 10 years and die after two years, the payments to a nominated beneficiary would continue for eight years.

- payments fixed at the same amount throughout your life – a level annuity, or payments to be lower than a level annuity to start with but rise over time by set amounts – an escalating annuity – or in line with inflation – an inflation-linked annuity.

- value protection – less commonly used and likely to reduce the amount of income you receive, but designed to pay your nominated beneficiary the value of the pot used to buy the guaranteed lifetime income less income already paid out when you die.

Investment-linked annuities

If you're willing to take more risk in return for a potentially higher income, you could opt for an income that is investment-linked (known as an investment-linked annuity). The income you receive rises and falls in line with the value of investments that you choose when you purchase your product. So, while it could pay more over the longer term than a basic annuity, your income could also fall.

Many investment-linked annuities guarantee a minimum income if the fund's performance is weak. With investment-linked annuities you can also have a dependant's pension, guarantee periods, value protection and higher rates if you have a short life expectancy due to poor health or lifestyle. Some investment-linked annuities allow you to change your investment options or allow you to take lower payments later.

Although you can't change your guaranteed income back into a pension pot, the government announced changes which came into force in early 2017, that allow you to sell your product for a cash lump sum on which you may have to pay Income Tax. How much tax you pay would depend on the value of your product, and your overall income in that year.

Think carefully about whether you need to provide an income for your partner or another dependant on your death. Consider whether you should take a product which provides an increasing income. Inflation (the general rise in price of goods and services over time) can significantly reduce your standard of living over time. Investment-linked annuities offer the chance of a higher income – but only by taking extra risk. Your income could reduce if the fund doesn't perform as expected. If you're considering this option look at what your provider can offer then get financial advice.

If you buy guaranteed income with money from a pension pot you've already used for another income option (e.g., to provide a flexible retirement income) you can't take a further tax-free lump sum – even if you chose not to take a tax-free lump sum with the other option.

Not all pension schemes and providers offer guaranteed lifetime income products. Some may only offer one type or offer to buy one on your behalf. Whatever the case, shop around before deciding who to go with – you're likely to get a better income than sticking with your current provider.

Tax

You will have to pay tax on the income you receive, in the same way you pay tax on your salary. How much you pay depends on your total income and the Income Tax rate that applies to you. Your provider will take tax off your income before you receive it

Because they won't know your overall income, they will use an emergency tax code to start with. This means you may pay too much tax initially and must claim the money back – or you may owe more tax if you have other sources of income. If the value of all of your pension savings is above £1,073,100 (2023-24 tax year) and these savings haven't already been assessed against the Lifetime allowance, further tax charges may apply when you access your pension pot.

Tax relief on future pension savings

After buying a guaranteed income product you can in most cases continue to get tax relief on pension savings of up to the Annual allowance of £60,000. However, if you buy a lifetime annuity which could decrease such as an investment-linked annuity, the maximum future defined contribution pension savings that can be made in a year that qualifies for tax relief is limited to the lower of £10,000 (the Money purchase annual allowance) or 100% of your earnings. If you want to carry on saving into a pension this option may not be suitable.

On death, if you have a single life guaranteed income product and no other features, your pension stops when you die. Otherwise, the tax rules vary depending on your age as shown below.

If you die before age 75: Income from a joint guaranteed income product will be paid to your dependant or other nominated beneficiary tax-free for the rest of their life. If you die within a guarantee period the remaining payments will pass tax-free to your nominated beneficiary then stop when the guarantee period ends. Any lump sum payment due from a value protected guaranteed lifetime income product will be paid tax-free. It will also normally fall outside your estate for Inheritance Tax purposes.

If you die age 75 or over: Income from a joint guaranteed income product or a continuing guarantee period will be added to the beneficiary's overall income and taxed at the appropriate Income Tax rate. Joint payments will stop when your dependant or other beneficiary dies and any guarantee period payments stop when the guarantee period ends.

Any lump sum due from a value protected guaranteed income product will be added to the beneficiary's overall income and taxed at the appropriate Income Tax rate. Lump sums due from a value protected guaranteed income product normally fall outside your estate for Inheritance Tax purpose.

3. Use your pension pot to provide a flexible retirement income
You can move all or some of your pension pot into an investment specifically designed to provide an income for your retirement . The income isn't guaranteed but you have flexibility to make   changes. This is sometimes called 'Flexi-access drawdown'.

You can choose to take up to 25% (a quarter) of your pension pot as a tax-free lump sum (up to £268,275). You then move the rest within six months into one or more funds (or other assets) that allow you to take income at times to suit you – e.g., monthly, quarterly, yearly, or irregular withdrawals. Most people use it to take a regular income. If you don't move the rest of your money within the six months, you'll be charged tax (normally 55% of the un-transferred fund value). Once you've taken your tax-free lump sum, you can start taking the income right away, or wait until a later date. The income is taxable.

Unlike with a guaranteed income for life (a lifetime annuity), the retirement income you receive from a flexible retirement income product is not guaranteed to last as long as you live, so you should think carefully about how much you withdraw.

Deciding how much income you can afford to take needs careful planning – it depends on how much money you put in from your pension pot, the performance of the funds, what other sources of income you have, and whether you want to provide for a dependant or someone else after you die. It also depends on how long you will live. Your retirement income could fall or even run out if you take too much too soon and start eating into the money you originally invested to produce the income – especially if stock markets fall. Investment choice is key

– you will need to review where your money is invested regularly to ensure it continues to meet your long-term retirement income needs. Investments can fall as well as rise – you'll need to know how you'll cope if your income suddenly drops.

Not all pension schemes and providers offer flexible retirement income products. If yours doesn't, you can transfer your pension pot to another provider who does but again there may be a fee to do so. Different providers will offer different features and charging structures on their products – and the choice is likely to increase.

You pay tax on the income withdrawals (outside the tax-free cash allowance). How much tax you pay depends on your total income and the Income Tax rate that applies to you. Your provider will take tax off your income payments in advance. Because they won't know your overall income, they will use an emergency tax code to start with which means you may initially pay too much tax – and must claim the money back – or you may owe more tax if you have other sources of income. If you have other income, you'll need to plan carefully how much flexible retirement income to take, to avoid pushing yourself into a higher tax bracket.

Tax relief on future pension savings

Once you have taken any money from your flexible retirement income product, the maximum future defined contribution pension savings that can be made in a year that qualifies for tax relief is limited to the lower of £4,000 (the Money purchase annual allowance – down from the usual £60,000 Annual allowance in 2023-24) or 100% of your earnings. If you want to carry on building up your pension pot, this may influence when you start taking your flexible retirement income. The tax relief you get for future pension savings is not affected if you take the tax-free lump sum but no income. On death, any remaining flexible retirement income funds when you die normally fall outside your estate for Inheritance Tax purposes.

If you die before age 75: Anything remaining in your fund passed to a nominated beneficiary within two years of notifying the provider of the pension holder's death will be tax-free whether they take it as a lump sum or as income. If it is over two years any money paid will be added to the beneficiary's income and taxed at their appropriate rate.

If you die age 75 or above: Anything remaining in your fund that you pass on – either as a lump sum or income – will be taxed at the beneficiary's appropriate Income Tax rate.

4. Take your pension pot as a number of lump sums

You can leave your money in your pension pot and take lump sums from it when you need it, until your money runs out or you choose another option.

You take cash from your pension pot as and when you need it and leave the rest invested where it can continue to grow tax-free. For each cash withdrawal the first 25% (quarter) will be tax-free and the rest is taxable. There may be charges each time you make a cash withdrawal and/or limits on how many withdrawals you can make each year. Unlike with the flexible retirement income option your pot isn't re-invested into new funds specifically chosen to pay you a regular income.

This option won't provide a regular income for you, or for any dependant after you die. Your pension pot reduces with each cash withdrawal. The earlier you start taking money out the greater the risk that your money could run out – or what's left won't grow sufficiently to generate the income you need to last you into old age.

Remember, as we saw in chapter 2, the buying power of cash reduces because of rising prices over time (inflation) – using cash sums to fund your long-term retirement isn't advisable. If you plan to use cash withdrawals to make a one-off purchase or to pay down debts, you must also be sure that you have enough left to live on for the rest of your life.

In addition, it is worth noting that this option won't provide a regular retirement income for you or for any dependants after you die.

Not all pension providers or schemes offer the ability to withdraw your pension pot as a number of lump sums. Shop around if you want this option but can't get it with your current provider, as charges and restrictions will vary. You may not be able to use this option if you have primary protection or enhanced protection, and protected rights to a tax-free lump sum of more than £268,275 (protections that relate to the Lifetime Allowance).

Tax

Three-quarters (75%) of each cash withdrawal counts as taxable income. This could increase your tax rate when added to your other income. How much tax you pay depends on your total income and the Income Tax rate that applies to you. Your pension scheme or provider will pay the cash and take off tax in advance. Because they won't know your overall income, they will use an emergency tax code to start with. This means you may pay too much tax and must claim the money back – or you may owe more tax if you have other sources of income. If the value of all your pension savings is above £1,073,100 and these savings haven't already been assessed against the Lifetime allowance (2023-24 tax year), further tax charges may apply when you access your pension pot. Once you reach age 75, if you have less remaining Lifetime allowance available than the amount you want to withdraw, the amount you will get tax-free will be limited to 25% (a quarter) of your remaining Lifetime allowance, rather than 25% of the amount you are taking out.

Tax relief on future pension savings

Once you have taken a lump sum, the maximum future defined contribution pension savings that can be made in a year that qualifies for tax relief is limited to the lower of £4,000 (the Money purchase annual allowance – down from the £60,000 Annual allowance for most people in 2023-24) or 100% of your earnings. If you want to carry on saving into a pension, this option may not be suitable.

On death any untouched part of your pension pot normally falls outside your estate for Inheritance Tax purposes.

If you die before age 75: Any untouched part of your pension pot will pass tax-free to your nominated beneficiary provided the money is claimed within 2 years of notifying the provider of the pension holder's death. If it is over 2 years the money will be added to the beneficiary's other income and taxed at the appropriate rate.

If you die age 75 or over: Any untouched part of your pension pot that you pass on - either as a lump sum or income - will be added to the beneficiary's overall income and taxed at the appropriate Income Tax rate.

5. Take your pension pot in one go

You no longer must convert your pension pot into an income if you don't want to. You can take out all your pension savings in one go if you wish. Cashing in your pension pot will not give you a secure retirement income. Basically, you close your pension pot and withdraw it all as cash. The first 25% (quarter) will be tax-free and the rest will be taxable.

This option won't provide a regular income for you – or for your spouse, civil partner, or other dependant after you die. Three-quarters (75%) of the amount you withdraw is taxable income, so there's a strong chance your tax rate would go up when the money is added to your other income. If you choose this option, you can't change your mind – so you need to be certain that it's right for you. For many or most people it will be more tax efficient to consider one or more of the other options. If you plan to use the cash to clear debts, buy a holiday, or indulge in a big-ticket item you need to think carefully before committing to this option.

Doing so will reduce the money you will have to live on in retirement, and you could end up with a large tax bill. In addition, you may not be able to use this option if you have primary protection or enhanced protection, and protected rights to a tax-free lump sum of more than £268,275 (protections that relate to the LIfetime Allowance). It is best to talk to your scheme if you have one or more of these kinds of protection and find out what your options are. There may be charges for cashing in your whole pot. Check with your scheme or provider. Not all pension schemes and providers offer cash withdrawal – shop around then get financial advice if you still want this option after considering its risks, as charges may vary.

Tax relief on future pension savings

Once you have cashed in your pension pot, the maximum future defined contribution pension savings that can be made in a year that qualifies for tax relief is limited to the lower of £4,000 (the Money purchase annual allowance – down from the usual £60,000 Annual allowance which will apply for most people in 2023-24) or 100% of your earnings.

On death, whatever age you die, any money remaining or investments bought with cash taken out of your pension pot will count as part of your estate for Inheritance Tax. By contrast, any part of your pot that was untouched would not normally be liable.

6. Mixing your options

You don't have to choose one option – you can mix and match as you like over time or over your total pension pot, whichever suits your needs. You can also keep saving into a pension if you wish and get tax relief up to age 75.

Which option or combination is right for you will depend on:

- when you stop or reduce your work
- your income objectives and attitude to risk
- your age and health
- the size of your pension pot and other savings
- any pension or other savings of your spouse or partner, if relevant
- the possible effect on your entitlement to State benefits
- whether you have financial dependants
- whether your circumstances are likely to change in the future.

Tax-free lump sums when mixing options

Note that depending on how you access money from your pension pot you may only get one chance to take your tax-free amount. This can be anything up to 25% (a quarter) of the amount you access and must be taken at that time. For example, if you use your whole pension pot to provide a flexible retirement income, you use up your rights to take a tax-free sum at the time you transfer the funds. So, whether you choose to take 25% tax-free, or less – or no tax-free sum at all – you can't take a tax-free lump sum later if, for example, you decide to use part of your flexible retirement income fund to buy a guaranteed income for life (an annuity). However, if you only used part of your pot to buy a flexible retirement income and later wanted to use some or all the remaining part of your pension pot to buy a regular income for life (a lifetime annuity), you could take up to 25% of that money as tax-free cash, subject to the limits of 2023.

On death, the same rules apply for passing on your remaining pension as already set out for each option.

Chapter 15

Reaching Retirement

We have discussed many of the issues in this section in previous chapters. Nevertheless, it is worth reiterating them as when you reach retirement age you will want to know the practical issues such as how do you claim your pension.

On reaching retirement age, it will be necessary to ensure that all paperwork relating to pension contributions is in order. There are a number of rules that should be observed in order to ensure that any pension due is paid:

- keep all documents relating to pension rights
- start organising any pension due before retirement, this will ensure that any problems are overcome well before retirement.

It is very important that communication is kept with all pension providers, and that they have accurate up-to-date records of a person's whereabouts. Each time addresses are changed this should be communicated to all pension providers. If it is impossible to track down an old employer from whom a pension is due, the Pension Schemes Registry can help. The Pensions Regulator is responsible for the Pension Schemes Registry. This was set up in 1990, by the government to help people trace so-called 'lost pensions'. If help is needed this can be obtained by filling in a form which can be accessed on the website of the pension's regulator www.pensionsregulator.gov.uk

How to claim state pension

A letter will be sent to all retirees about four months before retirement date. This will come from the pension service and will detail how much pension is due. The pension is not paid automatically, it must be claimed. This can be done by phoning the Pensions Claim Line number included with the letter, or by filling in a claim form BR1. If the person is a married man and the wife is claiming based on the husbands' contributions, then form BF225 should be filled in. If the pension is to be deferred it is advisable to contact the Pensions Service in writing as soon as possible at www. pensionsadvisoryservice.org.uk. A late pension claim can be backdated up to twelve months. If a man is claiming for a pension for his wife based on his contributions this can only be backdated six-months.

How the pension is paid

Pensions are paid by the DWP pension direct to a bank account or Post Office Card Account. To find out more about the payment of pensions contact the DWP www.gov.uk/government/organisations/department-for-work-pensions.

Leaving the country

If a person goes abroad for less than six months, they can carry on receiving pension in the normal way. If the trip is for longer then the Pension Service should be contacted and one of the following arrangements can be made to pay a pension: Have it paid into a personal bank account while away; arrange for it to be paid into a Post Office Card Account; arrange for the money to be paid abroad; If a person is living outside of the UK at the time of the annual pension increase they won't qualify for the increase unless they reside in a member country of the European Union or a country with which the UK has an agreement for increasing pensions. It is very important that you check what will happen to your state pension when you move abroad. The DWP International Pension Centre can help on 0191 218 7777, or access advice through their main website www.gov.uk/international-pension-centre.

Pensions from an occupational scheme
Although different schemes have different arrangements, there are similar rules for each scheme. About three months before a person reaches normal retirement age, they should contact the scheme. Either telephone or write enclosing all the details that they will need. The following questions should be asked:

- What pension is due?
- What is the lump-sum entitlement?
- How will the pension be reduced if a lump sum is taken?
- How will the pension be paid, will there be any choices as to frequency?
- Is there a widow's or widowers' pension, and if so how will it affect the retirement pension?
- Are there any pensions for other dependants in the event of death?

If a person has been making Additional Voluntary Contributions, then a detailed breakdown of these will be needed.

A pension from a personal plan

In the same way as a pension from an occupational scheme, it is necessary to get in touch with the pension provider about 3-4 months before retirement date.

The main questions that should be asked are:

- How much is the pension fund worth?
- How much pension will the plan provider offer?
- Can an increase be arranged each year and if so how much is the increase?
- What is the maximum lump sum?
- Is there a widow's or widowers or other dependants' pension?
- What are the other options if any?
- Can the purchase of an annuity be deferred without affecting the drawing of an income?

Pensions can only be paid by an insurance company or a friendly society so if the pension has been with any other form of provider, then it has to be switched before it can be paid.

If there are protected rights from a contracted-out pension plan, these can be, may have to be, treated quite separately from the rest of a pension. Protected rights from a personal pension cannot be paid until a person has reached 60 years of age. A person must, by law, have an open market option enabling protected rights pension to be paid by another provider, if it is desired.

New regulations for pension providers

As we have discussed, at the end of February 2015, the government introduced new regulations that pension providers must abide by. Pension providers will have to give specific risk warnings to savers looking to take advantage of the 2015 reforms. Any regulated company that sells policies that offer a retirement income will have to tell customers about the tax implications of cashing in or investing their pension once the reforms are fully enacted from April 6th, 2015. Pension companies must also highlight how a savers health could affect their retirement income. The providers must also provide advice on the effect on benefits and warn of scams.

Advice schemes for pensions

To help people with the transition, the government introduced a new advice service called Pension Wise, a service now administered through Money Helper (2023).

This was administered through The Pensions Advisory Services (TPAS) and the Citizens Advice Bureau. This was rolled out in March and April 2015 and has now merged into the Money and Pensions Service. Pensioners with defined contribution pension savings-either a workplace money purchase plan or a personal pension plan-will be able to access the scheme. They should be 55 or over or near retirement and can register through the Money Helper website www.moneyhelper.org.uk.

Customers will have to book an appointment to receive either phone-based advice or one to one advice and the sessions will last up to 45 minutes. Guidance will include life expectancy, long term care needs, various pension products from annuities to drawdown and a tax calculator. The guidance is not the same as regulated financial advice, such as how to invest your money but is general guidance.

Beware of Scams

As we all know, there are scammers in every walk of life. This is how they make their living, usually having failed in legitimate enterprise. There have been warnings of increased scamming activity since the chancellor first announced the changes. Basically, scammers cold call people, promising to unlock pensions, luring people with promises of sky-high returns on a number of ludicrous schemes, such as investment in property etc. In reality they are running off with your cash, leaving you with a sky-high tax bill and no money.

The fundamental rule is:

avoid any cold callers and those who promise anything at all. Avoid looking for free advice on the internet. **It is all bogus**. Manage your money yourself, after taking advice and guidance from the government scheme or through a financial advisor who is regulated by the Financial Conduct Authority. Always make sure that you are aware of the level of fees charged by financial advisors, as sometimes they can be quite high. Don't feel that you have to rush in if you are over 55. Take your time and consider the options carefully.

The Pensions Dashboard

At the time of writing (2023) the government is still working on the proposed pensions dashboard. This will be an extremely useful site when it materialises which will enable workers and retirees to see all their pension's details, both private and state pensions, on one website. For more information concerning the pensions dashboard and its progress go to www.pensionsdashboardsprogramme.org.uk.

Inheriting pensions on death

One important factor is the question of to whom do you leave your pension on death? Are your retirement policies updated in relation to who gets your pensions or is there a danger of the pension being passed on to the wrong person, such as an ex-husband or boyfriend or someone else who you would not like to see receive the pension?

The rise in the number of divorces, remarriages and couples co-habiting, plus a general apathy towards dealing with pensions when retirement is decades away, means many people could inadvertently be handing valuable benefits to former partners.

Pension schemes typically have a form that allows members to name the person they want their benefits to go to when they die "expressions of wishes".

Make sure that all your details are updated to ensure that any benefits go to the person you want them to go to!

****

Useful Organisations

Association of Investment Companies (AITC)
9th Floor
24 Chiswell Street
London
EC1Y 4YY
www.theaic.co.uk
020 7282 555

Debt Management Office
UK Debt Management Office
The Minster Building
21 Mincing Lane
London
EC3R 7AG
United Kingdom
0207 862 6500
www.dmo.gov.uk

Department for Work and Pensions (DWP)
If you ring The Pension Service on 0800 731 7898,
You will be connected to the pension centre covering your area,
Or you can look on the website (www. Thepensionservice.gov.uk

Disability Rights UK
www.disabilityrightsuk.org
Provides advice and publications on for disabled people.

The Financial Ombudsman Service
Exchange Tower
London E14 9SR
Consumer helpline: 0800 023 4567
www.financialombudsman.org,uk

Financial Conduct Authority (FSA)
12 Endeavour Square,
London,
E20 1JN.
0800 111 6768
www.fca.gov.uk

HM Revenue & Customs (HMRC)
The government department that deals
with almost all the taxes due in the UK.
Most HMRC leaflets can be obtained
from local tax offices or Tax Enquiry Centres
(look for in the phone book under `Revenue'
or `Government Department')
or Jobcentre Plus offices.

Almost all are also available on the website at:
https://www.gov.uk/government/collections/hm-revenue-and-customs-leaflets-factsheets-and-booklets

International Pension Centre
Tel: 0191 218 7777

Money and Pension Service
Tel: 0800 138 7777
www.moneyandpensionservice.org.uk

Moneyfacts
www.moneyfacts.co.uk

Office of the Public Guardian
The Office of the Public Guardian (OPG) protects people in England and Wales who may not have the mental capacity to make certain decisions for themselves, such as about their health and finance.
www.gov.uk/government/organisations/office-of-the-public-guardian

Pension Tracing Service
www.thepensionservice.gov.uk

Tax Help for Older People
Pineapple Business Park
Salway Ash
Bridport
Dorset DT6 5DB
Tel: 01308 488066 www.taxvol.org.uk

KEEPING ACTIVE

Association of British Travel Agents (ABTA)
30 Park Street
London SE1 9EQ

Te: 020 3117 0599

www.abtanet.com

British Franchise Association

www.thebfa.org

Community volunteering

Do-It-Trust (GB)

www.do-it.org

Cycling UK

www.cyclinguk.org

Department for Transport

Mobility inclusion

https://www.gov.uk/government/organisations/department-
for-transport

Disabled Persons Railcard Office

http://www.disabledpersons-railcard.co.uk

**European Health Insurance
Card (EHIC)**

http://www.nhs.uk/NHSEngland/Healthcareabroad

Learndirect

For free advice about all

Areas of learning and Training.

www.learndirect.com

Mobility-Motability Car Scheme
Tel: 0300 456 4566
www.motability.co.uk

National Association of Councils for Voluntary And Community Action
The Workstation,
Paternoster Row,
Sheffield
S1 2BX
0114 278 6636
www.motability.co.uk

National Federation of Women's Institutes
104 New Kings Road
London SW6 4LY
Tel: 020 7371 9300
www.thewi.org.uk

The Learning and Work Institute
www.learningandwork.org.uk
Tel: 020 7582 7221

National Trust
www.nationaltrust.org.uk

Open University (OU)
www.open.ac.uk

Age UK
0800 055 6112
www.ageuk.org.uk

Ramblers' Association
Tel: 020 3961 3300
www.ramblers.org.uk

Ramblers Scotland
Caledonia House
1 Redheughs Rigg
South Gyle
Edinburgh
EH12 9DQ
Tel: 0131 357 5850
Email: scotland@ramblers.org.uk

Ramblers Cymru
3 Coopers Yard
Curran Road
Cardiff
CF10 5NB
Tel: 020 3961 3310
Email: cerddwyr@ramblers.org.uk

**The Third Age Employment
Network (TAEN)**
207-221 Pentonville Road,
London

N1 9UZ,
Tel: 020 7843 1590

Voluntary Service Overseas (VSO)
145 London Road,
Kingston-Upon-Thames,
KT2 6QJ,
United Kingdom
020 8780 7500
www.vsointernational.org

Walking Women
Walking Women Ltd,
The Annex
143-1455 Stanwell Road
Ashford
Middlesex
TW15 3QN
Tel: 01784 664063
www.walkingwomen.com

NCVO (Working for a Charity)
8 Regents Wharf
London N1 9RL
020 7713 6161
www.ncvo.org.uk

RUNNING YOUR HOME

Abbeyfield Society
The Abbeyfield Society,
Hampton House,
17-19 Hampton Lane
Solihull
B912QJ
01727 857 536
www.abbeyfield.com

Almshouse Association
Tel: 01344 452922
www.almshouses.org

Pet Travel Scheme(PETS)
www.gov.uk/take-pet-abroad/overview

Living Made Easy (Disabled Living Foundation)
www.livingmade easy.org.uk
Tel: 0300 123 3084

Elderly Accommodation Counsel (EAC)
www.eac.org.uk

Federation of Master Builders (FMB)
David Croft House
25 Ely Place
London, EC1N 6TD

Tel: 0330 333 7777

www.fmb.org.uk

Foundations (the national co-ordinating
Body for home improvement agencies)

www.foundations.uk.com

Trust Mark

www.trustmark.org.uk

STAYING HEALTHY

Versus Arthritis

Helpline: 0300 790 0400

www.versusarthritis.org

Breast Cancer Care

www.breastcancersupport.org.uk

0300 80 80 900

(Oral) Health Foundation

Tel: 01788 546345

www.dentalhealth.org.uk

Diabetes UK

Wells Lawrence House,

126 Back Church Lane, London E1 1FH

Tel: 0345 123 2399

www.diabetes.org.uk

Institute of Trichologists
10 Harley Street
London
W1G 9PF
Telephone: 020 4532 6465
www.trichologists.org.uk

Keep Fit Association
www.keepfit.org.uk

**Royal Osteoporosis
Society (NOS)**
Manor Farm
Skinners Hill Camerton Bath BA2 OPJ
Helpline: 0808 800 0035
www.theros.org.uk

NHS Choices advice
www.nhs.uk

Patients Association
0800 345 7115
www.patients-association.org.uk

**Royal National Institute of
BLIND People (RNIB)**
0303 123 9999
www.rnib.org.uk

Royal National Institute for
Deaf People (RNID)
0808 808 0123
https://rnid.org.uk/

DEVELOPING-RELATIONSHIPS
British Association for Counselling and Psychotherapy (BACP)
Tel: 01455 883300
www.bacp.co.uk

Humanists UK
Humanists UK,
39 Moreland Street,
London
EC1V 8BB.
0207 324 3060
www.humanists.uk

Carers UK
20 Great Dover Street
London SE1 4LX
Carersline: 0207 378 4999
www.carersuk.org

Cruse-Bereavement Care
Helpline: 0808 808 1677
www.cruse.org.uk

Family Rights Group
101 Pentonville Road
London N1 9LG
0808 801 0366
www.frg.org.uk

Kinship (Formerly Grandparents' Plus)
0300 123 7015
www.kinship.org.uk

Relate
www.relate.org.uk

Home Care Association
020 8661 8188
www.homecareassociation.org.uk

Royal Voluntary Service
0808 196 3646
www.royalvoluntaryservice.org.uk

****

Index

Occupational pensions, 96, 116
Occupational Therapists, 60
Office of the Public Guardian, 92
Open and Distance Learning Quality Council, 14
Open College of Arts, 13
Open Ended Investment Companies (OEICs, 131

Passport, 53
Pension credit, 59
Pension Credit, 47
Pension Credit Guarantee, 65
Pension credits, 107
Pension Protection Fund, 135
Pension Tracing Service, 135
Pensioners Income Series, 94, 97
Pension-led funding, 132
Pensions, 3, 168
Pensions Advisory Services (TPAS), 165
Pensions Regulator, 161
Personal pensions, 96
Planning ahead for care, 72
Planning for the future, 93
Power of attorney, 90
Private pension, 96

RADAR, 25
Radio, 11
REACH, 17
Relate, 8, 16, 179
Repairs, 39
Retired and Senior Volunteer Programme, 17
Retirement due to ill-health, 134
Retirement housing, 29, 30, 67

****